Mystical Poems of Rūmī 2

This book was originally published by **Bibliotheca Persica** as number 23 in their Persian Heritage Series, edited by Ehsan Yarshater.

The Persian Heritage Series aims at making the best of Persian literary, historical, and scientific texts available in the major world languages. The translations in the series are intended not only to satisfy the needs of the students of Persian history and culture, but also to respond to the demands of the intelligent reader who seeks to broaden his intellectual and artistic horizons through an acquaintance with major world literature.

Bibliotheca Persica consists of the Persian Heritage Series, the Persian Studies Series, the Persian Art Series, and the Modern Persian Literature Series; and is prepared by the Center for Iranian Studies at Columbia University.

Mystical Poems of Rūmī 2

Second Selection, Poems 201-400

translated from the Persian by
A.J. Arberry

Edited by Ehsan Yarshater

The University of Chicago Press
Chicago and London

Published by arrangement with Bibliotheca Persica

The University of Chicago Press, Chicago 60637
The University of Chicago Press, Ltd., London
©1979 by Ehsan Yarshater
All rights reserved. Originally published in 1979 as No. 23 in
    the Persian Heritage Series
University of Chicago Press edition 1991
Printed in the United States of America

08 07 06 05 04 03 02 01 00 99   6 7 8 9 10

Library of Congress Cataloging in Publication Data

Jalāl al-Dīn al-Rūmī, Maulana, 1207-1273.
    Selections. English. 1991
    Mystical poems of Rumi : second selection, poems 201-400
/ translated from the Persian by A.J. Arberry ; edited by
Ehsan Yarshater.
        p. cm.
    Reprint. Originally published: New York : Bibliotheca
Persica, 1979.
        ISBN 0-226-73152-9 (pbk.)
    1. Jalāl al-Dīn al-Rūmī, Maulana, 1207-1273—Translations
into English. 2. Sufi poetry, Persian—Translations into
English.
I. Arberry, A.J. (Arthur John), 1905-1969. II. Yar-Shater,
Ehsan.
III. Title.
PK6480.E5A7   1991
891'.5511-dc20   91-14060
                                                            CIP

♾ The paper used in this publication meets the minimum
requirements of the American National Standard for
Information Sciences—Permanence of Paper for Printed
Library Materials, ANSI Z39.48-1992.

Contents

Transcription Notes   vi

Foreword by E. Yarshater   vii

Autobiographical sketch by A.J. Arberry   ix

Translation: Poems 201-400   1

Notes   147

Bibliography   178

Transcription

The transcription system used here for Persian and for Arabic elements in Persian, aims at simplicity and accuracy, and has been jointly adopted by Corpus Inscriptionum Iranicarum, Encyclopaedia Persica, the Persian Heritage Series, the Persian Studies Series, Bibliothèque Persane, and Meisterwerke der persischen Literatur.

	Persian	Arabic		Persian	Arabic		Persian	Arabic
ء	'		ض	ż	ḍ	Vowels		
ب	b		ط	ṭ		آ ا	ā	
پ	p		ظ	ẓ		ایٰ	à	
ت	t		ع	'		و	ū	
ث	s̱	t̲	غ	ḡ		ی	ī	
ج	j		ف	f		---	a	
چ	č		ق	q		'	o	
ح	ḥ		ک	k		---	e	(but iy)
خ	ḵ		گ	g		◄	e, a	a
خو	ḵᵛ		ل	l		وَ	ow	aw
د	d		م	m		یَ	ey, ay	ay
ذ	z̲	d̲	ن	n				
ر	r		و	v	w			
ز	z		ه	h				
ژ	ž		ی	y				
س	s							
ش	š							
ص	ṣ							

Note:
The more familiar and commonly used place names, titles when not an integral part of the name, and other commonly known words have been anglicized without diacritics for the sake of simplicity (e.g., shah, Isfahan, Turkman, khan, etc.).

Foreword

In 1963, I suggested to the late Professor Arberry that he undertake the translation of a representative selection of Rūmī's lyrics from the *Dīvān-e Shams,* to be published in the Persian Heritage Series. Rūmī's *Dīvān,* despite its somewhat uneven texture, contains some of the most inspiring poems written in the Persian language and has certainly not been surpassed in the sheer depth and exuberance of feeling by the work of any other Persian poet. And yet the *Dīvān* had remained largely untranslated into English. R. A. Nicholson's *Selected Poems from the Dīvāni Shamsi Tabrīzī,* (Cambridge University Press, 1898) which contained the translation of forty-eight lyrics, was the most extensive work to represent the *Dīvān* in English.

Professor Arberry, with his exemplary knowledge of Persian literature, his vast experience in translating literary works, and his personal affinities with mystical thought of the poet, was the outstanding choice for the handling of this most difficult task. Rūmī, although easy to enjoy in Persian, is far from easy to translate. Much of the appeal of his poetry depends on the musicality of his verse, which is bound to be lost in translation. The force of his passion and the subtlety of his mystical sentiments, expressed in a somewhat unorthodox diction, is also a constant challenge to the translator.

Professor Arberry's translation of the first two hundred poems was ready in 1965 and was published jointly by Allen and Unwin and the University of Chicago Press in 1968 under the title of *Mystical Poems of Rūmī, I.*[1]

After the publication of the first volume, Professor Arberry, afflicted with failing health, nevertheless was able to complete, though with great difficulty, the preparation of the present volume, which contains translations of another two hundred poems. His untimely death in 1973, which dealt a serious blow to Persian and Arabic studies, came before he was able to send me his manuscript and it was only through the diligence and kindness

[1]A paperback edition of the same was published by the University of Chicago Press in 1972.

of his daughter that the manuscript was located and placed at my disposal.

The reading of Professor Arberry's once fine and legible handwriting, however, proved a major task. Fortunately Dr. Hasan Javadi, a former and loyal student of his and now Professor and Chairman of the English Department at the University of Tehran, kindly agreed to prepare the manuscript for typing, collate it with the original, and also annotate the translation, following the pattern set by Professor Arberry in the first volume. Without his dedicated assistance the publication of this volume could not have been accomplished.

This volume is prefaced by what is perhaps the most intimate writing of Professor Arberry on his training, his spiritual journey, and his intellectual outlook. It throws light on the inner thought and sentiments of a distinguished humanist and scholar.

It is my pleasant task to thank Mr. M. Kasheff and Dr. D. Bishop of Columbia University, and Professor Gh. Youssefi of the University of Mashhad for their assistance in resolving some of the ambiguous points in the translation. The editors, however, have not allowed themselves, except in a few necessary cases, to alter the text of the translation, which remains basically the same as left by the translator.

It is hoped that the two volumes, now made available, will prove of assistance to the students of Rūmī and an incentive to them for a complete translation of his *Dīvān*.

Ehsan Yarshater
Columbia University, 1978

An Autobiographical Sketch by the Late Professor A. J. Arberry*

I was born the child of Victorian parents, strict believers of the Christian evangelical school. My early religious education was therefore of the same pattern: family prayers, church three times every Sunday, a severe puritanical attitude to pleasure, especially on the Lord's Day. My parents were virtuous and, according to their lights, deeply sincere in their conformity; they were poor, but being industrious and thrifty they spared their children the full rigors of poverty only too prevalent in England at the beginning of the present century. They were also ambitious for their children, determined that they should benefit to the full from the rapidly improving educational opportunities of those times. I attended elementary school from the age of three, won a scholarship to the local grammar school, and from there proceeded in due course to Cambridge. My education had cost my parents only the expense of feeding and clothing me; but that was a sufficiently large sacrifice to the poor of their generation, and I cannot adequately express my thankfulness to them for their love and devotion and unfailing encouragement.

When the first war broke out I was nine years old: my father served in the Royal Navy, and saw his brother's ship go down with all hands at the Battle of Jutland. The years 1914–18 were terribly anxious years for naval families; they were also fearful years for children as the technique for bombing civilians advanced, but they were incomparably easier than the years 1939–45 in which my own child grew up. The early 1920s were a time of disillusionment and doubt. For us in Britain the war had been won, but the peace was obviously lost: many thousands of heroes returned to unemployment; the poor became poorer still. These were the years in which, along with perhaps the majority of my contemporaries, I lost faith—the faith, that is, which I had been taught by my parents. Being what is called a clever boy, I read voraciously the rationalists, the agnostics, the atheists; I was persuaded that the mind was the measure of all things; I applied my reason to the dogmas of Christianity, and my reason rejected

*This *Apologia Spiritualis* was found among Professor Arberry's papers.

them. Having at one time seriously thought of the priesthood, I now abandoned worship entirely and resolved to become an academic scholar, abstract truth being the only altar before which I would kneel.

By a paradox which would have delighted Shaw whose writings had done so much to destroy my childhood beliefs, it was this resolution which ultimately led to the restoration of my faith. I graduated in classics, and then, disappointed at the narrow field of research offered by those ancient studies, I decided in a hasty moment to become an orientalist and chose for my particular course Arabic and Persian. I suppose it amused the unbeliever in me that I would henceforward be devoting my mind to a critical examination of Islam, no doubt as fallacious as Christianity. It certainly never occurred to me that that examination would have the effect of bringing me back to a belief in God.

In 1926, while still an undergraduate, I had attended the funeral of Edward Glanville Browne. It was a studentship established under his will that enabled me in 1927 to embark on my new studies. My teachers were Anthony Ashley Bevan, a Victorian agnostic who was a splendid philologist and a most kindly man, and Reynard Alleyne Nicholson, the eminent authority on Islamic mysticism. My encounter with Nicholson was the turning point in my life. He was at that time engaged on his last and greatest work, the editing and translating of the *Maṣnavī* of Jalāl al-dīn Rūmī; and when I was ready to undertake research in Arabic and Persian, he persuaded me to follow in his footsteps and to explore the rich literature of the Sufis. My first labor was to edit and translate the *Mavāqef* of al-Neffārī, and this led to my first journey to the East and three years' residence in the lands of Islam. In those years I married and became a father.

Nicholson was a very shy and retiring man, painfully diffident —a scholar of the study who never traveled out of Europe, yet he achieved a deeper penetration of the mind and spirit of Islam than any other man I have ever known. He rarely spoke of his personal beliefs, and in/twenty-five years of close friendship I learned little of his own spiritual formation. But the impression I gained was that he too had lost his faith as a young man, and had regained it through his intellectual communion with the mystics of Islam. In his old age he composed a poem in which he revealed for the first time his inner thoughts. These thoughts had obviously been profoundly influenced by his long studies of Rūmī.

Deep in our hearts the Light of Heaven is shining
    Upon a soundless Sea without a shore.
Oh, happy they who found it in resigning
    The images of all that men adore.

Blind eyes, to dote on shadows of things fair
    Only at last to curse their fatal lure,
Like Harut and Marut, that Angel-pair
    Who deemed themselves the purest of the pure.

Our ignorance and self-will and vicious pride
    Destroy the harmony of part and whole.
In vain we seek with lusts unmortified
    A vision of the One Eternal Soul.

Love, Love alone can kill what seemed so dead,
    The frozen snake of passion. Love alone,
By tearful prayer and fiery longing fed,
    Reveals a knowledge schools have never known.

God's lovers learn from Him the secret ways
    Of Providence, the universal plan.
Living in Him, they ever sing His praise
    Who made the myriad worlds of Time for Man.

Evil they knew not, for in Him there's none;
    Yet without evil how should good be seen?
Love answers: "Feel with me, with me be one;
    Where I am nought stands up to come between."

There are degrees of heavenly light in souls;
    Prophets and Saints have shown the path they trod,
Its starting points and stages, halts and goals,
    All leading to the single end in God.

Love will not let his faithful servants tire,
  Immortal Beauty draws them on and on
From glory unto glory drawing nigher
  At each remove and loving to be drawn.
When Truth shines out words fail and nothing tell;
Now hear the Voice within your hearts. Farewell.

I have spoken at this length of my old friend, whom I saw last
very shortly before his death in 1945, because I am conscious of
a debt to Nicholson which I can never hope to repay. He was the
perfect scholar, so devoted to his books that he blinded himself
by reading, so modest and humble that he was totally unaware
of his greatness. It was an old man with failing sight who penned
these lines which for me contain the surest revelations and the
most moving of last men's eyes:

When Truth shines out words fail and nothing tell;
Now hear the Voice within your hearts. Farewell.

It was of that serene vision of Truth that al-Ḥallāj, the great Mus-
lim mystic, spoke shortly before his crucifixion in 922:

Now stands no more between the Truth and me
  Or reasoned demonstration,
  Or proof or revelation;
Now, brightly blazing full, Truth's luminary,
  That drives out of sight
  Each flickering, lesser light.

"What is Truth?" asked jesting Pilate of the Man whom he
would presently give on a like Cross, the Man who said, "I am
the Way, the Truth and the Life." I have said earlier that as a
young man, having abandoned formal worship, I resolved to
become an academic scholar, abstract truth being the only altar
before which I would kneel. In those days I supposed truth to be
a thing intellectually attainable, a quest for reason, far removed
from the emotions. But the mystical affinity of truth with light
was evidently already apprehended by Sir William Jones, that
greatest of British orientalists who died in 1794 and whose ex-
ample has always been my chief inspiration. Jones wrote:

Before thy mystic altar, heavenly Truth,
I kneel in manhood, as I knelt in youth.
There let me kneel, till this dull form decay,
And life's last shade be brightened by thy day;
Then shall my soul, now lost in clouds below,
Without consuming glow.

Truth, then, is Light—a light that shines into the heart. And what is light? The answer seems to be given in that sublime verse of the Qur'an:

God is the light of the heavens and the earth;
    the likeness of His Light is as a niche
        wherein is a lamp
        (the lamp in a glass,
    the glass as it were a glittering star)
        kindled by a Blessed Tree,
    an olive that is neither of the East nor of the West
whose oil well-nigh would shine, even if no fire touched it.
    Light upon Light,
God guides to His Light whom He will.

Once this light has shone into the heart, no darkness can ever overcome it. I believe that light to be a reality, because I have myself experienced it. I believe it also to be the Truth, and I think it not inappropriate to call it God. I am an academic scholar, but I have come to realize that pure reason is unqualified to penetrate the mystery of God's light, and may, indeed, if too fondly indulged, interpose an impenetrable veil between the heart and God. The world in which we live is certainly full of shadows. I have had my full share of personal sorrows and anxieties, and I am as acutely aware as the next man of the appalling dangers threatening mankind. But because I have experienced the Divine Light, I need not wish for any higher grace.

I have now for some years resumed my Christian worship, in which I find great comfort, being no longer troubled by the intellectual doubts generated by too great a concern for dogma. I know that Jew, Muslim, Hindu, Buddhist, Parsi—all sorts and conditions of men—have been, are and will always be irradiated by that Light "kindled by a Blessed Tree, an olive that is neither of the East nor of the West"—the universal tree of the Truth and Goodness of God. For God, being the One Universal, has an infinite solicitude and love of each particular, and suffers His Light to shine into every human heart open to receive it.

201

The ravings which my enemy uttered I heard within my heart; the secret thoughts he harbored against me I also perceived.

His dog bit my foot, he showed me much injustice; I do not bite him like a dog, I have bitten my own lip.

Since I have penetrated into the secrets of individuals like men of God, why should I take glory in having penetrated his secret?

I reproach myself that through my doubtings it so happened that purposely I drew a scorpion towards my own foot.[1]

Like Eblīs who saw nothing of Adam except his fire, by God I was invisible to this insignificant Eblīs.

Convey to my friends why I am afflicted in mind; when the snake bit my thigh I started away from the black rope.

The blessed silent ones, their lips and eyes closed—by a way unknown to any man, I ran into their thoughts;

Since there is a secret and perfect way from heart to heart, I gathered gold and silver from the treasuries of hearts.

Into the thought that was like a brazen stove I flung the dead dog; out of the thought that was like a rose bower I plucked roses and jasmine.

If I have hinted at the evil and good of my friends, I have spun flax like a weaver as the choicest veil.

When my heart rushed suddenly to a heart mighty and aware, out of awe for his heart I fluttered like the heart.

As you are happy with your own state, how did you fall in with me? Attend to your own business, for I am neither shaikh nor disciple.

As far as you are concerned, brother, I am neither copper nor red gold; drive me from your door, for I am neither lock nor key.

Take it as if I had not ever spoken these words; if you had been in my mind, by God I would not have quarreled.

202

I closed my eyes to creation when I beheld his beauty, I became intoxicated with his beauty and bestowed my soul.

For the sake of Solomon's seal I became wax in all my body,

and in order to become illumined I rubbed my wax.[2]

I saw his opinion and cast away my own twisted opinion; I became his reed pipe and likewise lamented on his lip.

He was in my hand, and blindly I groped for him with my hand; I was in his hand, and yet I inquired of those who were misinformed.

I must have been either a simpleton or drunk or mad that fearfully I was stealing from my own gold.

Like a thief I crept through a crack in the wall into my own vine, like a thief I gathered jasmine from my own garden.

Enough, do not twist my secret upon your fingertips, for I have twisted off out of your twisted fist.

Shams-e Tabrīz, from whom comes the light of moon and stars—though I am grieving with sorrow for him, I am like the crescent of the festival.

203

Reason says, "I will beguile him with the tongue"; Love says, "Be silent. I will beguile him with the soul."

The soul says to the heart, "Go, do not laugh at me and your-self. What is there that is not his, that I may beguile him thereby?"

He is not sorrowful and anxious and seeking oblivion that I may beguile him with wine and a heavy measure.

The arrow of his glance needs not a bow that I should beguile the shaft of his gaze with a bow.

He is not prisoner of the world, fettered to this world of earth, that I should beguile him with gold of the kingdom of the world.

He is an angel, though in form he is a man; he is not lustful that I should beguile him with women.

Angels start away from the house wherein this form is, so how should I beguile him with such a form and likeness?

He does not take a flock of horses, since he flies on wings; his food is light, so how should I beguile him with bread?

He is not a merchant and trafficker in the market of the world that I should beguile him with enchantment of gain and loss.

He is not veiled that I should make myself out sick and utter sighs, to beguile him with lamentation.

I will bind my head and bow my head, for I have got out of hand; I will not beguile his compassion with sickness or fluttering.

Hair by hair he sees my crookedness and feigning; what's hidden from him that I should beguile him with anything hidden.

He is not a seeker of fame, a prince addicted to poets, that I should beguile him with verses and lyrics and flowing poetry.

The glory of the unseen form is too great for me to beguile it with blessing or Paradise.

Shams-e Tabrīz, who is his chosen and beloved—perchance I will beguile him with this same pole of the age.

204

My mother was fortune, my father generosity and bounty; I am joy, son of joy, son of joy, son of joy.[3]

Behold, the Marquis of Glee has attained felicity; this city and plain are filled with soldiers and drums and flags.

If I encounter a wolf, he becomes a moonfaced Joseph; if I go down into a well, it converts into a Garden of Eram.[4]

He whose heart is as iron and stone out of miserliness is now changed before me into a Ḥātem of the age in generosity and bounty.[5]

Dust becomes gold and pure silver in my hand; how then should the temptation of gold and silver waylay me?

I have an idol such that, were his sweet scent scattered abroad, even an idol of stone would receive life through joy.

Sorrow has died for joy in him of "may God bind your consolation"; how should not such a sword strike the neck of sorrow?

By tyranny he seizes the soul of whom he desires; justices are all slaves of such injustice and tyranny.

What is that mole on that face? Should it manifest itself, out of desire for it forthwith maternal aunt would be estranged from paternal [uncle].

I said, "If I am done and send my story, will you finish it and expound it?" He answered, "Yes."

_,05

When I am asleep and crumbling in the tomb, should you come to visit me, I will come forth with speed.

You are for me the blast of the trumpet and the resurrection, so what shall I do? Dead or living, wherever you are, there am I.

Without your lip I am a frozen and silent reed; what melodies I play the moment you breathe on my reed!

Your wretched reed has become accustomed to your sugar lip; remember wretched me, for I am seeking you.

When I do not find the moon of your countenance, I bind up my head [veil myself in mourning]; when I do not find your sweet lip, I gnaw my own hand.

206

The time has come for us to become madmen in your chain, to burst our bonds and become estranged from all;

To yield up our souls, no more to bear the disgrace of such a soul, to set fire to our house, and run like fire to the tavern.

Until we ferment, we shall not escape from this vat of the world—how then shall we become intimate with the lip of that flagon and bowl?

Listen to the words from a madman: do not suppose that we become true men until we die.

It is necessary that we should become more inverted than the tip of a comb in the top of the twisted tress of felicity;

Spread our wings and pinions like a tree in the orchard, if like a seed we are to be scattered on this road of annihilation.

Though we are of stone, we shall become like wax for your seal; though we be candles, we shall become a moth in the track of your light.

Though we are kings, we shall travel straight as rocks for your sake, that we may become blessed through your queen on this chessboard.

In the face of the mirror of love we must not breathe a word of ourselves; we must become intimate with your treasure when we are changed to waste.

Like the tale of the heart we must be without head or ending, that we may become dwellers in the heart of lovers like a tale.

If he acts the seeker, we shall attain to being sought; if he acts the key, we shall become all the wards of the lock.

If Moṣṭafā does not make his way and couch in our hearts, it is meet that we should lament and become like the Wailing Column.[6]

No, be silent; for one must observe silence towards the watchman when we go towards the pavilion by night.

207

Last night my soul cried, "O exalted sphere of heaven, you hang indeed inverted, with flames in your belly.

"Without sin and crime, eternally revolving, upon your body in its complaining is the deep indigo of mourning;[7]

"Now happy, now unhappy, like Abraham in the fire; at once king and beggar like Ebrāhīm-e Adham.[8]

"In form you are terrifying, yet your state is full of anguish: you turn round like a millstone and writhe like a snake."

Heaven the blessed replied, "How should I not fear that one who makes the Paradise of the world as Hell?

"In his hand earth is as wax, he makes it Zangī and Rūmī, he makes it falcon and owl, he makes it sugar and poison.[9]

"He is hidden, friend, and has set us forth thus patent so that he may become concealed.

"How should the ocean of the world be concealed under straws? The straws have been set adancing, the waves tumbling up and down;

"Your body is like the land floating on the waters of the soul; your soul is veiled in the body alike in wedding feast or sorrow.[10]

"In the veil you are a new bride, hot-tempered and obstinate; he is railing sweetly at the good and the bad of the world.

"Through him the earth is a green meadow, the heavens are unresting; on every side through him a fortunate one pardoned and preserved.

"Reason a seeker of certainty through him, patience a seeker of help through him, love seeing the unseen through him, earth taking the form of Adam through him.

"Air seeking and searching, water hand-washing, we Messiah-like speaking, earth Mary-like silent.

"Behold the sea with its billows circling round the earthy ship; behold Kaabas and Meccas at the bottom of this well of Zamzam!"[11]

The king says, "Be silent, do not cast yourself into the well, for you do not know how to make a bucket and a rope out of my withered stumps."

208

Every day I bear a burden, and I bear this calamity for a purpose:

I bear the discomfort of cold and December's snow in hope of spring.

Before the fattener-up of all who are lean, I drag this so emaciated body;

Though they expel me from two hundred cities, I bear it for the sake of the love of a prince;

Though my shop and house be laid waste, I bear it in fidelity to a tulip bed.

God's love is a very strong fortress; I carry my soul's baggage inside a fortress.

I bear the arrogance of every stonehearted stranger for the sake of a friend, of one long-suffering;

For the sake of his ruby I dig out mountain and mine; for the sake of that rose-laden one I endure a thorn.

For the sake of those two intoxicating eyes of his, like the intoxicated I endure crop sickness;

For the sake of a quarry not to be contained in a snare, I spread out the snare and decoy of the hunter.

He said, "Will you bear this sorrow till the Resurrection?" Yes, Friend, I bear it, I bear it.

My breast is the Cave and Shams-e Tabrīzī is the Companion of the Cave.[12]

209

If I weep, if I come with excuses, my beloved puts cotton wool in his ears.

Every cruelty which he commits becomes him, every cruelty which he commits I endure.

If he accounts me nonexistent, I account his tyranny generosity.

The cure of the ache of my heart is the ache for him; how shall I not surrender my heart to his ache?

Only then are glory and respect mine, when his glorious love renders me contemptible.

Only then does the vine of my body become wine, when the wine-presser stamps on me and spurns me underfoot.

I yield my soul like grapes under the trampling, that my secret heart may make merry,

Though the grapes weep only blood, for I am vexed with this cruelty and tyranny.

He who pounds upon me puts cotton wool in his ears saying, "I do not press unwittingly.

"If you disbelieve, you are excusable, but I am the Abu'l Ḥikam [the expert] in this affair.[13]

"When you burst under the labor of my feet, then you will render much thanks to me."

210

I have got out of my own control, I have fallen into unconsciousness; in my utter unconsciousness how joyful I am with myself!

The darling sewed up my eyes so that I might not see other than him, so that suddenly I opened my eyes on his face.

My soul fought with me saying, "Do not pain me"; I said, "Take your divorce." She said, "Grant it"; I granted it.

When my mother saw on my cheek the brand of your love she cut my umbilical cord on that, the moment I was born.[14]

If I travel to heaven and read the Tablet of the Unseen, O you who are my soul's salvation, without you how I am ruined![15]

When you cast aside the veil the dead became alive; the light of your face reminded me of the Covenant of Alast.[16]

When I became lost, O soul, through love of the king of the peris, hidden from self and creatures, I am as if peri-born myself.

I said to the Tabriz of Shams-e Dīn, "O body, what are you?" Body said, "Earth"; Soul said, "I am distraught like the wind."

211

Without you, Darling, in both worlds I have seen no joy; many wonders I have seen, a wonder like you I have not seen.

They said, "The blaze of fire will be the infidel's portion"; none have I seen exempted of your fire save Bū Lahab.[17]

I have oft laid the ear of my soul at the window of the heart; I have heard much discourse, but I have seen no lips.

Suddenly you scattered compassion on your servant; I saw no cause for that save your infinite tenderness.

Chosen *sāqī*, apple of my eyes, the like of you never appeared in Persia, in Arabia I never saw.

Be lavish with that wine whose juice never came to festive gathering and that glass the equal of which I saw not in Aleppo.[18]

Pour wine in such abundance that I set out a foot from myself, for in selfhood and existence I have seen only weariness.

You who are sun and moon, you who are honey and sugar, you who are mother and father, no lineage have I seen but you.

O infinite love, O divine manifestation, you are both stay and refuge; an epithet equal to you I have not heard.

We are iron filings and your love is the magnet; you are the source of all questing, in your quest none I have seen.

Be silent, brother, dismiss learning and culture; till you recited culture, no culture in you I saw.

Shams-e Ḥaqq-e Tabrīz, source of the source of souls, without the Baṣra of your being, no date have I ever known.[19]

212

Lord, what a Beloved is mine! I have a sweet quarry; I possess in my breast a hundred meadows from his reed.

When in anger the messenger comes and repairs towards me, he says, "Whither are you fleeing? I have business with you."

Last night I asked the new moon concerning my Moon. The moon said, "I am running in his wake, my foot is in his dust."

When the sun arose I said, "How yellow of face you are!" The sun said, "Out of shame for his countenance I have a face of gold."

"Water, you are prostrate, you are running on your head and face." Water said, "Because of his incantation I move like a snake."

"Noble fire, why do you writhe so?" Fire said, "Because of the lightning of his face my heart is restless."

"Wind-messenger of the world, why are you light of heart?" Wind said, "My heart would burn if the choice were mine."

"Earth, what are you meditating, silent and watchful?" Earth said, "Within me I have a garden and spring."

Pass over these elements, God is our succorer; my head is aching, in my hand I hold wine.

If you have barred sleep to us, the way of intoxication is open. Since I have one to assist, he offers wine in both hands.

Be silent, that without this tongue the heart may speak; when I hear the speech of the heart, I feel ashamed of this speech.

213

Weary not of us, for we are very beautiful; it is out of very jealousy and proper pride that we entered the veil.

On the day when we cast off the body's veil from the soul, you will see that we are the envy and the despair of man and the Polestars.

Wash your face and become clean for beholding us, else remain afar, for we are beloveds of ourselves.

We are not that beauty who tomorrow will become a crone; till eternity we are young and heart-comforting and fair of stature.

If that veil has become worn out, the beauty has not grown old; the life of the Veil is transient, and we are boundless life.

When Eblīs saw the veil of Adam, he refused; Adam called to

him, "You are the rejected one, not I."

The rest of the angels fell down prostrate, saying as they bowed themselves, "We have encountered a beauty:

"Beneath the veil is an idol who by his qualities robbed us of reason, and we, prostrate, fell."

If our reason does not know the forms of the foul old men from those of the beauties, we are apostates from love.

What place is there for a beauty? For he is the Lion of God. Like a child we prattled, for we are children of the alphabet.

Children are beguiled with nuts and raisins, else, how are we meet for nuts and sesame-grains?

When an old woman is hidden in helmet and chainmail, she says, "I am the illustrious Rostam of the battle ranks."

By her boast all know that she is a woman; how should we make a mistake, seeing that we are in the light of Aḥmad?[20]

"The believer is discriminating"—so said the Prophet; now close your mouth, for we are guided rightly without speech.[21]

Hear the rest from Shams the Pride of Tabriz for we did not take the end of the story from that king.

214

Rise, lovers, that we may go towards heaven; we have seen this world, so let us go to that world.

No, no, for though these two gardens are beautiful and fair, let us pass beyond these two, and go to that Gardener.

Let us go prostrating to the sea like a torrent, then let us go foaming upon the face of the sea.

Let us journey from this street of mourning to the wedding feast, let us go from this saffron face to the face of the Judas tree blossom.[22]

Trembling like a leaf and twig from fear of falling, our hearts are throbbing; let us go to the Abode of Security.

There is no escape from pain, since we are in exile, and there is no escape from dust, seeing that we are going to a dustbowl.

Like parrots green of wing and with fine pinions, let us become sugar-gatherers and go to the sugar-bed.

These forms are signs of the signless fashioner; hidden from the evil eye, come, let us go to the signless.

It is a road full of tribulation, but love is the guide, giving us instruction how we should go thereon;

Though the shadow of the king's grace surely protects, yet it is better that on that road we go with the caravan.

We are like rain falling on a leaky roof; let us spring from the leak and go by that waterspout.

We are crooked as a bow, for the string is in our own throats; when we become straight, then we will go like an arrow from the bow.

We cower like mice in the house because of the cats; if we are lion's whelps, let us go to that Lion.

Let us make our soul a mirror in passion for a Joseph; let us go before Joseph's beauty with a present.

Let us be silent, that the giver of speech may say this; even as he shall say, so let us go.

215

Did I not say to you, "Go not there, for I am your friend; in this mirage of annihilation I am the fountain of life?"[23]

Even though in anger you depart a hundred thousand years from me, in the end you will come to me, for I am your goal.

Did I not say to you, "Be not content with worldly forms, for I am the fashioner of the tabernacle of your contentment?"

Did I not say to you, "I am the sea and you are a single fish; go not to dry land, for I am your crystal sea?"

Did I not say to you, "Go not like birds to the snare; come, for I am the power of flight and your wings and feet?"

Did I not say to you, "They will waylay you and make you cold, for I am the fire and warmth and heat of your desire?"

Did I not say to you, "They will implant in you ugly qualities so that you will forget that I am the source of purity to you?"

Did I not say to you, "Do not say from what direction the servant's affairs come into order?" I am the Creator without directions.

If you are the lamp of the heart, know where the road is to the house; and if you are godlike of attribute, know that I am your Master.

216

Bring wine, for I am suffering crop sickness from the vintage; God has seized me, and I am thus held fast.

By love's soul, bring me a cup of wine that is the envy of the sun, for I care for aught but love.

Bring that which if I were to call it "soul" would be a shame, for the reason that I am pained in the head because of the soul.

Bring that whose name is not contained in this mouth, through which the fissures of my speech split asunder.

Bring that which, when it is not present, I am stupid and ignorant, but when I am with it, I am the king of the subtle and crafty ones.

Bring that which, the moment it is void of my head, I become black and dark, you might say I am of the infidels.

Bring that which delivers out of this "bring" and "do not bring"; bring quickly, and repel me not, saying, "Whence shall I bring it?"

Bring, and deliver the roof of the heavens through the long night from my abundant smoke and lamentations.

Bring that which after my death, even out of my dust, will restore me to speech and thanksgiving even as Najjār.[24]

Bring me wine, for I am guardian of wine like a goblet, for whatever has gone into my stomach I deliver back completely.

Najjār said, "After my death would that my people might be open-eyed to the ecstasy within me.

"They would not regard my bones and blood; in spirit I am a mighty king, even though in body I am vile.

"What a ladder I, the Carpenter, have chiseled! My going has reached the roof of the seventh heaven.

"I journeyed like the Messiah, my ass remained below; I do not grieve for my ass, nor am I asslike of ears.

"Do not like Eblīs see in Adam only water and clay; see that behind the clay are my hundred thousand rose bowers."

Shams-e Tabrīzī rose up from this flesh saying, "I am the sun. Bring up my head from this mire.

"Err not, when I enter the mire once more, for I am at rest, and am ashamed of this veil.

"Every morning I will rise up, despite the blind; for the sake of the blind I will not cease to rise and set."

217

What hidden sweetness there is in this emptiness of the belly!
Man is surely like a lute, no more and no less;[25]

For if, for instance, the belly of the lute becomes full, no
lament high or low will arise from that full lute.

If your brain and belly are on fire through fasting, because of
the fire every moment a lament will arise from your breast.

Every moment you will burn a thousand veils by that fire; you
will mount a hundred steps with zeal and endeavor.

Become empty of belly, and weep entreatingly like the reed
pipe; become empty of belly, and tell secrets with the reed pen.

If your belly is full at the time of concourse, it will bring Satan
in place of your reason, an idol in place of the Kaaba.

When you keep the fast, good habits gather together before
you like slaves and servants and retinue.

Keep the fast, for that is Solomon's ring; give not the ring to
the *dīv*, destroy not your kingdom.

Even if your kingdom has gone from your head and your army
has fled, your army will rise up, pennants flying above them.

The table arrived from heaven to the tents of the fast, by the
intervention of the prayers of Jesus, son of Mary.

In the fast, be expectant of the table of bounty, for the table of
bounty is better than the broth of cabbages.

218

I have a fire for you in my mouth, but I have a hundred seals
on my tongue.

The flames which I have in my heart would make one mouthful of both worlds.

Though the entire world should pass away, without the world
I possess the kingdom of a hundred worlds.

Caravans which are loaded with sugar I have in motion for
the Egypt of nonexistence.

The drunkenness of love makes me unaware whether I have
profit or loss therefrom.

The body's eye was scattering pearls because of love, till now I have a pearl-scattering soul.

I am not housebound, for like Jesus I have a home in the fourth heaven.[26]

Thanks be to Him who gives soul to the body; if the soul should depart, yet I have the soul of the soul.

Seek from me that which Shams-e Tabrīzī has bestowed, for I have the same.

219

By the God who was in pre-eternity living and moving and omnipotent, everlasting,[27]

His light lit the candles of love so that a hundred thousand secrets became known.

By one decree of Him the world was filled—lover and loved, ruler and ruled.

In the talismans of Shams-e Tabrīzī the treasure of His marvels became concealed.

For from the moment that you journeyed forth, we became separated from sweetness like wax;

All the night we are burning like candles, paired to his flame and deprived of honey.

In separation from his beauty my body is a waste, and the soul in it is like an owl.

Turn those reins in this direction, twist the trunk of the elephant of joy.

Without your presence concert is not lawful; music has been stoned like Satan.

Without you not one ode has been uttered, until that gracious vision of yours arrived and was understood;

Then out of the joy of hearing your letter five or six odes were composed.

May our eventide through you be radiant dawn, O you in whom Syria and Armenia and Rūm glory.[28]

220

Heart pure of breath and firm of foot, you came in order to warn the best of communities.

Only at the direction of the heart you set your head like a pen on the page of eternal love.[29]

In joy at your air and your justice we are dancing like a pennant.

Master, whither are you going, dancing? Towards liberation and the place of the plain of nonexistence.

Master, say, which nonexistence in this? The ear of eternity knows the letter of eternity.

Love is a stranger, and his tongue is strange, like that Arab stranger in Persia.[30]

Rise up, for I have brought you a tale; give ear to your servant neither more nor less;

Give ear to this strange speech; the tale is strange, and the speaker too.

From the face of that Joseph the bottom of the well became bright and happy as the Garden of Eram;

That prison became a palace with orchards and meadows, Paradise, and a royal hall and vestibule of sanctity.

As when you fling a clod into the water, the water that very moment parts open;

Like a night of cloud, when the sun of dawn suddenly puts up its head from the well of grief;

Like the wine which the Bedouin drank and said, "God bless its jar and praise God";[31]

Out of the joy of this imprisonment in humiliation and loss he [Joseph] looks upon the high-exalted heaven.

Reason be not envious of my mouth; God has born witness and counted the blessings.

Though the tree drinks hidden water, there is clearly seen on its branches what it has concealed.

Whatever the earth has stolen from heaven, it yields up honestly in the season of spring.

Whether you have stolen a bead or a jewel, whether you have hoisted a flag or a pen,

Night has departed, and lo, your day has arrived; the sleeper shall see that which he has dreamed of.

221

Stealthily as the soul, you are going in the midst of my soul; O luster of my garden, you are my gracefully moving cypress.

When you go, go not without me; soul of my soul, go not without my body, and depart not out of my sight, O my blazing torch.

I bear up the seven heavens and pass beyond the seven seas, when lovingly you gaze into my giddy soul.[32]

Since you came into my bosom, infidelity and faith are my servitors, O you whose vision is my religion, whose face is my faith.

You have made me headless and footless; enter drunken and laughing, O my Joseph of Canaan.[33]

Through your grace I have become soul-like and have become hidden from myself, O you whose being has become hidden in my hidden being.

The rose rends its garment because of you, O you with whom the narcissus' eye is intoxicated, of whom the branches are pregnant, O you my infinite garden.

One moment you brand me, the next you draw me into the garden; you draw me before the lamp so that my eyes may be opened.

O soul before all souls, O mine before all mines, O moment before all moments, O my very own, O my very own!

Our resting place is not earth; though the body crumbles, it matters not. My thought is not the skies, O you, union with whom is my heaven.

The grave of mariners is the sea forevermore; in the water of life what is death, O you, my Sea, my Ocean?[34]

O you whose scent is in my sigh, whose sigh is my fellow traveler, in the hope of my Emperor color and scent have become distraught with me.[35]

My soul, since like a note in the air it has become separated from all heaviness, why should it be without you, O origin of my four elements?[36]

O my king Ṣalāḥ-al-dīn, you who know my way and see my way, you who are free of concern with my little dignity, loftier than my potentiality.[37]

222

Lovers, lovers, it is time to migrate from the world; the drum of departure is reaching my spirit's ear from heaven.

See, the driver has arisen, the camel train is arrayed, he has begged us for quittance; caravaners, why are you asleep?

These sounds ahead and behind are the sounds of departure and the camel-bells; every moment a soul and a breath is setting off into placelessness.

From these inverted candles, from these indigo veils, there issues a wondrous people that the things unseen may become visible.[38]

If heavy slumber fell upon you from this revolving sphere, alas for this light life! Beware of this heavy slumber!

Heart, depart to the Sweetheart; friend, depart to the Friend; watchman, be wakeful—a watchman should not sleep.

On every side are candles and torches, on every side noise and tumult, for tonight the pregnant world gives birth to the eternal world.

You were clay and became heart, you were ignorant and became intelligent; he who has drawn you on so far will draw you beyond [this world].

In drawing and drawing you his pains are delectable; his flames are like water, do not frown thereon.

His business is to dwell in the soul, his business to break penitence vows; by his abundant contrivance these motes are trembling at heart.[39]

Laughing stock, jumping out of your hole as if to cry, "I am the lord of the land," how long will you jump? Bend your neck, or they will bend you like a bow.

You sowed the seeds of deceit, you indulged in mockery, you deemed God nonexistent; now look, you cuckold!

Ass, you were apter for straw; a cauldron, you were better black; you were better at the bottom of the well, you disgrace to house and household!

In me there is Another from whom these angers leap; if water scalds, it is through fire—realize this!

I have no stone in my hand; I have no quarrel with anyone; I deal harshly with none, for I am gay as a rose bower.

My anger is therefore from that source, it is from the other world; this side a world, that side a world—I am seated on the threshold.

That man sits on the threshold who is mutely eloquent; you have uttered this hint, that is enough; say no more, draw back your tongue.

223

O gardener, gardener, autumn has come, autumn has come; see on branch and leaf the mark, see the mark of heart-anguish.

O gardener, attend, give ear, hearken to the lament of the trees; on every side a hundred tongueless ones, a hundred tongueless ones bewailing.

Never without cause are eyes weeping and lips parched; no one without heart-anguish is pale of cheek, pale of cheek.

In short, the raven of grief has entered the garden and is stamping his feet, demanding in mockery and oppression, "Where is the rose bower, where is the rose bower?

"Where is lily and eglantine? Where cypress and tulip and jasmine?

"Where the green-garmented ones of the meadow? Where the Judas tree, where the Judas tree?

"Where are the nurses of the fruits? Where the gratis honey and sugar? Every breast, every breast is dry of this flowing milk.

"Where is my sweet-voiced nightingale? Where is my cooing ringdove? Where is the peacock fair as an idol? Where are the parrots, where are the parrots?"

Like Adam having eaten a grain fallen from his abode, their crown and fine robes have flown from this dazzling array, this dazzling array.

The rose bower constrained like Adam, alike lamenting and expectant, since the Lord of Bounty said to them, "Do not despair."[40]

All the trees drawn up in ranks, black-robed, plunged in mourning, leafless and sad and lamenting because of that trial.

O crane and lord of the village, at last return some answer;

"Have you gone into the depths or departed to heaven, to heaven?"

They replied, "Enemy raven, that water shall return to the streams, the world will become full of scent even as Paradise, even as Paradise."

O babbling raven, be patient three months more, till there arrive despite you the festival of the world, the festival of the world.

Through the voice of our Seraphiel our lantern will become bright, we shall become alive from the death of that autumn festival, that autumn festival.[41]

How long this denial and doubt? Behold the mine of joy and salt; fly to heaven like a manikin without a ladder, without a ladder!

The beastlike autumn dies, you stamp upon its grave; lo, the dawn of fortune is breaking, O watchman, watchman!

O dawn, fill the world with light, drive afar these Hindus [of the night], set free the time, recite a spell, recite a spell![42]

O sweet-working sun, return to Aries, leave neither ice nor mud, scattering ambergris, scattering ambergris.

Fill the rose bower with laughter, bring to life those dead ones, make shining the concourse; ha, see what comes to sight.

The seeds are escaped from prison, we too from the corner of our houses; the garden out of hidden places has brought a hundred presents, a hundred presents.

The rose bower fills with beauties, fur coats are a drug on the market, the cycle of time, the cycle of time is giving birth and generating.

The crane is coming with his drooping wings over the palace, tall as the sky, babbling as if to say, "Yours is the kingdom, O refuge in need, O refuge in need!"

The nightingale enters playing the lute, and that dove cooing, the other birds celebrate with song, youthful fortune, youthful fortune.

I am pregnant with this resurrection; I abandon the speech of the tongue; the thoughts of my heart come not into the tongue, into the tongue.

Silence! Listen, father, to the news from garden and birds: flying arrowlike they have come from placelessness, from placelessness.

224

Enough now from the cry *doš*—"dismount"—I have remained far from my road; enough from the cry *qoš*—"set off"—I have missed my tent.[43]

When will you deliver me this *qoš*? When will you deliver me from this *doš*, that I may arrive at your prosperity, at my moon and threshing floor?

Though I am happy on this journey, over plain and mountain and valley, in your love, O sun of splendor, timely and untimely,

Yet where is the broad highway? Where is the sight and justice of the king? Especially for me, consumed in yearning for my king.

How long must I ask news of you from the zephyr? How long must I seek your moon's image in the water of my well?

I have been burnt up a hundred ways like the garden, and likewise I have learned from spring—in both states I am dumbfounded at the handiwork of my God.

225

I become not satiated with you—this is my only sin; be not satiated with compassion for me, O my refuge in both worlds!

Satiated and weary of me have become his jar, and water-carrier and waterskin; every moment my water-seeking fish becomes thirstier.

Break the pitcher, tear up the waterskin, I am going towards the sea; make clear my road.

How long will the earth become mire from my teardrops? How long will the sky be darkened by the grief and smoke of my sighs?

How long will my heart lament, "Alas, my heart, my ruined heart?" How long will my lips wail before the phantom of my king?

Go towards the sea from which the wave of delight is coming; behold how my house and hospice are drowned in its wave.

Last night the water of life surged from the courtyard of my house; my Joseph yesterday fell like the moon into my well.[44]

Suddenly the torrent came and swept all my harvest away;

smoke mounted from my heart, my grain and chaff were consumed.

Though my harvest is gone, I will not grieve; why should I grieve? The halo of the light of my moon is more than enough for a hundred like me.

He entered my heart; his image was of fire. The fire rose over my head; my cap was consumed.

He said, "Concerts impair dignity and respect." You can have dignity, for this love is my luck and dignity.[45]

I desire not intellect and wisdom; his learning is enough for me. The light of his cheek at midnight is the blaze of my dawn.

The army of sorrow is mustering; I will not grieve at his army because my horses, squadron on squadron, have seized even heaven.

After every ode my heart repents of discoursing; the summons of my God waylays my heart.

226

If any man asks you about the houris, show your face, saying, "Like this"; if any man speaks to you of the moon, get up onto the roof—"Like this."

If any seeks a peri, show him your countenance; if any mentions musk, open your tresses—"Like this."[46]

If any says to you, "How does cloud disclose the moon?," loosen knot by knot the strings of your gown—"Like this."

If one asks you how the Messiah revived the dead, before him kiss me on the lips—"Like this."

If any says to you, "Say, how is he who is slain of love?" exhibit to him my soul—"Like this."

If any asks you compassionately about my stature, exhibit your own brow folded double—"Like this."

The soul is separated from the body, and thereafter returns again; ho, show to those who disbelieve, enter the house—"Like this."

Whenever you hear a lover's lament, by God's right, all that is our story—"Like this."

I am the home of every angel, I am the black and blue beaten chest; raise your eyes and look well at heaven—"Like this."[47]

To none but the zephyr have I told the secret of union with the Beloved, so that the zephyr said in the joy of its secret heart—"Like this."

Despite him who says, "How shall the servant attain God?" put in the hand of every eye a bright candle—"Like this."

I said, "How does the scent of Joseph travel from city to city?" The scent of God breathed from the world of Hū—"Like this."[48]

I said, "How does the scent of a Joseph give back sight?" Your breeze irradiated my eyes—"Like this."

From Tabriz haply Shams-e Dīn will be benevolent, and out of his grace in fidelity lift up his head—"Like this."

227

Lord, would that I knew what is the desire of my Beloved; He has barred my road of escape, robbed me of my heart and my repose.

Lord, would that I knew whither He is dragging me, to what purpose He is dragging my toggle in every direction.

Lord, would that I knew why He is stonyhearted, that loving King of mine, my long-suffering Darling.

Lord, would that I knew whether my sighing and my clamor, "My Lord and my defense!"—will reach my Beloved at all.

Lord, would that I knew where this will end; Lord, this my night of writing is very long.

Lord, what is this ferment of mine, all this bashfulness of mine?—Seeing that you are mine, you are at once my one and my thousand.[49]

Your love is always both silent and eloquent before the image of my eye, my sustenance and my fate!

Now I call him quarry, now I call him spring, now I nickname him wine, now my crop sickness.

He is my unbelief and faith, my light-beholding eye, that of mine and this of mine—I cannot escape from him.

No more patience has remained for me, nor sleep, nor tears nor wrath; Lord, how long will he raid all the four of mine?

Where is the house of water and clay, compared with that of soul and heart? Lord, my sole desire has become my hometown and habitation.[50]

This heart is banished from the town, stuck in dark mire, lamenting, "O God, where is my family and retinue?"

Lord, if only I might reach my city and behold the companion of my Palace, and all that city of my friend!

Gone then my hard road, the heavy load from my back; my long-suffering Darling would come, carrying off my load.

My lion-catching deer would drink to the full of my milk, he whose quarry I am would have become my quarry.

Black-faced night is then not the mate and consort of my day; stonyhearted autumn follows not in the wake of my springtide.

Will you not be silent? How long will you beat this drum? Alas, my veiled lip, that you have become veil-rending!

228

Suddenly today the enemy of my penitence and patience approached me midway on the road and cherished me like a king.

Seizing a cup like any drunkard, in it a hundred blandishments and charms, he held before me the wine cup, saying, "If you are a winebibber, take."

Illumined as the face of Moses, blessed as Mount Sinai, gleaming as the White Hand, dilated with joy as the heart of 'Emrān.[51]

Ho, come take this clean tablet from this Moses; be not arrogant like Pharaoh, contend not like Hāmān.[52]

I said to him, "Moses, what is in your hand?" He said, "One time this is a staff, one time a serpent.[53]

"From every separate atom a hundred various shapes appear; for whatever is necessary for Bū Horaira is in the bag.[54]

"In my hand is the control of it, I change it into every form; I make poison into medicine, I make the difficult easy.

"Now I strike it on the sea and bring up dust from the sea; now I strike it on the rock and the fountain of life gushes out.

"Now I showed the limpid water of the Nile to the enemy as blood, to the common folk I showed stone and earth as pearl and coral.

"To the eye of the envious I am the wolf; to Jacob himself, Jospeh; to the ignorant, Bū Jahl; Moḥammad, before him who knows God."[55]

Sweet-breathed rosewater is death and asphyxiation to the

black beetle; sugary syrup is fatal to the bilious.[56]

Apparently all seekers are fellow travelers; in reality they are back to back. One has made his lodging in the lowest depths, the other in the highest heaven.

Like a child and an old man, though apparently fellow travelers, one is increasing every day, the other every moment on the decline.

What a cup of poison and candy is this! What magic and jugglery! This turn and this revolution keep you giddy.

The world is fixed and you see it as revolving; when a man's head is spinning, he sees the house as spinning.

Know as a station of fear that in which you are secure; know as a station of security that in which you tremble.

Since you are contrary and false you see everything contrariwise; foolish man, when you consult a woman, oppose her![57]

That one is a woman whose road and qibla is color and scent; truly woman is the evil-commanding soul in human form.[58]

The counsel of the spiritual is like the buzzing of bees; from its lip it fills the floor of the house to the attic with its sweets.[59]

Bravo the incomprehensible comprehended, bravo the familiar stranger, bravo the sourness better than sweet, bravo the unbelief better than faith!

Be silent, for the tongue has become a door keeper from measuring words; when the heart speaks without words, it occupies the high throne like a king.

Shine, Shams-e Tabrīzī, upon the Houses of the heart, for the sun of a secure seat is not like this spinning sun.[60]

229

My world-illuminating lamp is not shining so brightly; strange —is this the fault of the eye, or the light, or the window?

Has perchance the end of the thread become lost? What has become of that past state? In that state the tip of the needle does not remain hidden.

Happy the moment when the *farrāš* of "we spread" within this mosque pours oil from the olive of God into this lantern of the heart![61]

Heart, enter the crucible of fire, sit there quietly like a man, for through the influence of this fire the iron became such a mirror.

When Abraham entered the flames like gold coin, there grew from the face of the fire a jasminebed and roses and lilies.[62]

If you do not bring your heart out of this tumult into this passion, what will you do with this heart? Come, sit here and tell me.

If out of unmanliness you do not enter the ring of true men, be outside like a ring on men's door and knock.

Since the prophet said "Fasting is a protection," lay hold of that, do not cast away this shield before the arrow-shooting carnal soul.[63]

On this dry land a shield is necessary; when you reach the sea, then there will grow on your body a coat of mail like a fish to repel his shafts.

230

It is the rule with drunkards to fall upon one another, to fight and squabble and make tumult.

The lover is worse then the drunkard; the lover also belongs to that party. I will tell what love is; it is to fall into a goldmine.

What may that gold be? The lover is the king of kings; it means becoming secure from death and not caring for the golden crown.

The darvish in his cloak, and in his pocket the pearl—why should he be ashamed of begging from door to door?

Last night that moon came along, having flung his girdle on the road, so drunken that he was not aware that his girdle had fallen.

I said, "Leap up, my heart, place wine in the hand of the soul; for such a time has befallen, it is time to be roistering,

"To become hand in hand with the garden nightingale, to fall into sugar with the spiritual parrot."

I, heart-forlorn and heart-yielded, fallen upon your way—by Allāh, I know of no other place to fall.

If I broke your bowl, I am drunk, my idol. I am drunk—leave me not from your hand to fall into danger.

This is a newborn rule, a newly enacted decree—to shatter glasses, and to fall upon the glassmaker!

231

Go, know that the code of lovers is opposite to all other ways, for from the Beloved lies are better than truth and beneficence.

His impossibility comes to pass, his insalubriousness is a bonus, his injustice is all rectitude. Calumny from him is justice.

His hard is soft, his synagogue is the Kaaba, the Beloved's thorn is better than roses and basil.

The moment when he is bitter is better than a sweetshop, and the moment when he becomes weary, that is kissing and embracing.

The moment when he says to you, "By Allāh, I am indifferent to you"—that is the water of Khidr from the fountain of life.[64]

The moment when he says "No," in his "No" are a thousand "Yeses"; his strangerhood is kinship according to the code of the unselfed.

His infidelity becomes all faith, his stone all coral, his miserliness all beneficence, his crime all forgiveness.

If you criticize, you say, "You have a crooked way of going on"; I have bought the way of his brow and given my life.

I am drunk with this crooked way; I have made enough, and closed my lips—rise up, bright heart, and recite the rest of it.

Shams-al-Ḥaqq Tabrīzī! Dear Lord, what sugar you sprinkle! You might say that out of my mouth proceed a hundred proofs and demonstrations.

232

Become placeless in the Unity, make your place in the essence of annihilation; every head which possesses duality put on a Christian neck.

In the cage of being, before this bird of sanctity flies on the wing, make it sugar-cracking in thankfulness.

Since you were drunk in pre-eternity, seize the sword of post-eternity, like a Turk plunder the Hindu boy of existence.[65]

Filter and purify the dregs of your separate being, and fill that glass of true reality with pure wine.

So long as you are a snake of earth, how shall you be a fish of religion? Snake, when you have become a fish, then charge into the sea.

Observe the beast, how it holds its head towards the earth; if you are a man, why then, lift your head towards the heights.

When in Adam's school you have become intimate with God, sit on the high throne of the King and teach the Names.[66]

If you desire the kingship of *illā*, proceed first to *lā*; seize the broom from *lā* and become a sweeper of *things*.[67]

If you intend to journey, go on the mount of meaning, and if it be so that you take up residence, let it be in the green dome of heaven.

Be like the sufferer from dropsy who is never satiated; however high you get, strive to rise still higher.

Every spirit that has an aim keeps his face to the door; you aim at this madness, so turn your head towards madness.

The body is not without a shadow, and the shadow cannot be bright; fly towards the window and make your flight unaccompanied.

Following Majnūn's rule, be an agent of turmoil, for this love is declaring, "Make yourself quit of reason!"[68]

Become at once a burning fire, and become roasted and well-browned; become at once drunk and wine, seize fast without either.

Become at once secretive and intimate, be silent and become companion; at once become us and become ours, likewise be servant to us.

Lest the Christian should steal into your monastery, now be a lover of the girdle, now aim at the cross.[69]

You have become learned, but only in existential learning; go without existential eyes, make your eyes see.

A moses with the character of Khidr, Shams-al-Ḥaqq Tabrīzī —lay your head at his foot, seek the White Hand.[70]

233

Come, how much is a kiss from that precious ruby? If a kiss is for a life, it is a duty to buy.

Since the kiss is pure and not proper to earth, I will become a disengaged spirit, I will emerge from this body.

The sea of purity said to me, "No aspiration is granted gratis;

the pearl of price is with you—come, break the shell."

For a kiss of the rose, which confers splendor on wine, the whole world is putting out its tongue like a lily.

I blunder, if you be all kings, if you be like Mars and the moon, ask not for a kiss from that untamed Darling.

Enter, moon of heaven, for I have opened the window; for one night shine on my face, press your lips on mine.

Close the door of speech and open the heart's window; you will not obtain a kiss of this moon save by way of the window.

234

A call came to the soul from the sphere of the Pleiades: "Come up, do not sit below like the dregs."

No one remains so long on a journey apart from his homeland and former friends.

Well, you have heard the call, *Return* from that king and sweet emperor.[71]

In this ruined waste owls are dwelling; what habitation have you fashioned, poor falcon?

What rest does he get, on whichever side he turns, who makes his mattress of thorns?

What bond is there between money-changer and counterfeiter? What relation is there between crow and falcon?

Why do you adorn with plaster a ruin which above is covered with paintings and beneath is a prison?

Why do you not adorn your soul with wisdom? For its every word is worth a hundred Chinas and Māčīns; that wisdom which is the source of disputation is not that wisdom which causes the soul to see God.[72]

Become a jewel so that willy-nilly they will plant you altogether on the golden crown.

Be done with going back like a twisted foot; be as *alif*, sit single and upright.

Since meaning is a horse and words are as a saddle, say, how long will you draw along this saddle without the horse?

Throw clods at the love of men; you too are a man, but a man of clay;

The wedding of clay creature with clay creature brings a

shower of clods and stones for a dowry.

Look at the tombs beneath the bricks, for you cannot tell apart their heads from their foundations.

O God, bring my soul safely to the souls by that road on which the family of Yāsīn went;[73]

Mingle our prayers with theirs, so that from us comes the prayer and from Thee the amen.

Grant that thy grace and loving kindness may be such that, as little as our good works may be, from Thee comes the "Well done."

Bring us safely from lustfulness to reasonableness, unto the zenith above from this lower abode.

235

Whither would you fly from my clutch? Who knows how to rend the net of omnipotence?

Since you have not the foot to flee from me, bend down your neck, have done with obstinacy.

Run towards sweetness like unripe grapes, if you know not how to run inwardly.

Caught in the net you are biting the rope; this rope shall not be broken by biting.

Do you not see how your head is in my bowstring? You are a bow, you must bend to the string.

Why do you kick up your hind legs saying, "I have escaped the load?" I have merely let you go for a moment to graze.

In fear and awe of me the sea's heart surges with billows and throbbing.

If the rocky mountain should encounter that blow, it would not be able to leap out of my chains.

Until my command says to heaven, "Enough," it must go on spinning around my earth.

Desire is a milk from the teats of Satan; your reason is to suck asses' milk.

Earth's mouth is dry out of despair for me, without me it cannot swallow a single mouthful.

Who is able to attack my quarry? Who is able to purchase my slave?

He whom I have seized and chosen, whom shall he choose other than me?

The soul has no security save in love; it is necessary to creep amongst lovers.

Lovers have security in both worlds; even so they were at the time of creation.

It behooves not the sheep to scatter away from the shepherd towards the wolves because the shepherd is cruel.

This shepherd will not shed the blood of the sheep, for he knows to rear them to eternal life.

Know that the companions of the body are the Companions of the Elephant; how can such ever reach the Kaaba?[74]

For the Kaaba is the world's navel, the elephant is the nose; it is not possible to draw the nose to the navel.

Become as *abābīl*, and do not flee from the elephant; the heart is like *abābīl* in picking up grains.[75]

It plucks the enemy like grains, it knows to hear the message of the Kaaba.

Through the heart you will mount to the heavens, through the heart the rose of felicity will blossom;

Through the heart you will travel to the Beloved, through the heart you will escape the body's shame.

The heart has a cauldron cooked for your sake; wait patiently until it is cooked.

Shams-al-dīn Tabrīz is the heart of hearts; the bat is unable to see the sun.

236

See how every particle of the world is passing by, see how everyone has arrived from a journey;

See how everyone desirous of his own sustenance has bowed his head before his king.

See how, like the stars, for the sake of its glow, are all fallen helpless at the foot of the sun;

See how, like torrents in quest of water, all are tumbling headlong towards their sea.

See how for each from the king's kitchen a table is prepared according to his needs.

See how the sea of the world is contracted before this sea-drinking cup.

And as for those whose sustenance is the king's countenance, see how their mouths are filled with sugar of the king's beauty.

Behold with the eyes of Shams-e Tabrīzī; see another ocean filled with pearls.

237

This is love: to fly to heaven, every moment to rend a hundred veils;

At first instance, to break away from breath—first step, to renounce feet;

To disregard this world, to see only that which you yourself have seen.[76]

I said, "Heart, congratulations on entering the circle of lovers,

"On gazing beyond the range of the eye, on running into the alley of the breasts."

Whence came this breath, O heart? Whence came this throbbing, O heart?

Bird, speak the tongue of birds: I can heed your cipher!

The heart said, "I was in the factory whilst the home of water and clay was abaking.

"I was flying from the workshop whilst the workshop was being created.

"When I could no more resist, they dragged me; how shall I tell the manner of that dragging?"

238

That enemy of soul and mind and faith has returned, shaking his sleeves—

Blunderer of a hundred thousand houses, devastator of a hundred thousand shops,

Stirrer-up of a hundred thousand tumults, amazement-focus of a hundred thousand amazed ones,

That nurse of reason and bane of reason, that friend of the soul and enemy of the soul.

Whither will he transport my light reason? He seeks a reason like that of Loqmān.[77]

How does he accept my worthless soul? He seeks a soul like the sea of Oman.

He came, saying, "Bring the tribute of the village!" I said, "What village? It is a ruined village.

"Your flood has shattered cities; how shall a village stand amid the flood?"

He said, "Ruins are the abode of treasures; it is our ruin, O Muslim!

"Give us the ruin, or go forth; do not upbraid, do not speak at random."

The ruin is of yourself; once you have gone it thrives through the justice of the King.

Do not dissemble and say I have gone; do not hide behind the door.

Make yourself as one dead, that you may become living by the spirit of a man.

You said, "You shall not be in the midst"; that saying of yours is the essence of Qur'an.

The work you do, yourself not in the midst, that is work done by God—know this for sure.

I will recite the rest of the poem in secret; it cannot be told before the uninitiated.

Silence! For there are a hundred thousand differences between the tongue's utterance and the light of revelation.

239

Do not grieve over any joy that has gone forever, for it will return to you in another form, know that for sure.

Did not the child find joy in its nursing and in milk? When the child was weaned from milk, the joy came from wine and honey.

This joy is an unqualified thing which enters various forms, moves from box to box between water and clay;

It suddenly displays its grace in the water of the rain, again enters into the rosebed, and lifts its head from the earth.

Now it comes by water, now by way of bread and meat, now

by way of beauty, now by way of horse and saddle.

From behind these veils suddenly one day it peeps and shatters all the idols, that which is neither that nor this.[78]

The soul in sleep leaves the body and appears in a phantasm; the body is deposed and idle—in another form it is manifest.[79]

You might say, "In a dream I saw myself like a cypress, my face as a bed of tulips, my body as roses and jasmine."[80]

That phantasm of the cypress vanished, the soul returned to its house; *verily in this and that is a warning to all beings.*

I fear stirring up trouble, though I would have spoken what may be spoken, God speaks fairer than I—do not let go of the saddlestraps of the faith.

Fā'ilātun fā'ilātun fā'ilātun fā'ilāt, if you have not gold-wheat bread, yet speak the golden words.

At last, Tabriz of the soul, look upon the stars of the heart, that you may see this mundane sun to be a reflection of Shams-e Dīn.

240

My king of moonfaced ones went up to his sick lovers, saying, "O pale cheeks and saffronbed of mine!

"I will water my saffronbed, I will convert the saffron to roses with my fountain of life.

"Yellow and red, thorn and rose are at my control and command; set not your head save on the line of my command, my command!

"The world's rosefaced ones have stolen beauty from my beauty; they have stolen an atom of my beauty and beneficence.

"In the end these moonfaced ones are becoming strawfaced; that is the state of thieves in the presence of my King."

Day has come; earthly ones, restore the stolen goods. O my soul, whence come goods for earthly man, and whence beauty?

When at night the sun has vanished, the stars make boast. Venus says, "Know it is mine"; the moon says, "No, mine."

Jupiter produces Ja'far gold from his purse; Mars says to Saturn, "See my cutting dagger!"[81]

Mercury takes the high seat—"I am the Ṣadr-al-ṣodūr, the

heavens are my kingdom, the zodiacs are my pillars!"

With dawn the sun draws up his army from the east saying, "Thieves, where have you gone? See, it is mine!"

Venus is terrified, the moon's neck is broken; Mercury has become dry and cold with my shining face.

The business of Mars and Saturn is ruined by our light; Jupiter is bankrupt, saying, "Alas, my purse is gone!"

When the sun had run afield, came a cry, "Ho, mannerless one, get out of my field!

"I am the sun of the sun: sun, depart! Sink into the well of the west: enter my prison.

"At dawn lift your head from the east and come to life; make the desires of the resurrection aware of my proof.

"Every man's festival is the month [moon] to which he is a sacrifice; your festival is my month [moon], you who are a sacrifice to me!"[82]

When Shams-e Tabrīzī shone from the House of *not-of-the-East,* the glow of his essence surpassed my bounds and potentialities.[83]

241

The intellectual is all the time engaged in showing off; the lover is all the time becoming unselfed and distraught;

Intellectuals are running away, afraid of drowning; the whole business and trade of love is drowning in the sea.

Intellectuals find repose by contriving repose; lovers think it a shame to be attached to repose.

The lover will be in a circle, alone from everyone, just as oil and water, though in the same place, are separate.

The man who goes to the trouble of offering advice to lovers gets nothing for his pains but to be a mockery of passion.

Love has the scent of musk, it is therefore notorious; how can musk escape from such notoriety?

Love is like a tree, and lovers are the shade of that tree; though the shade fall afar, yet it must attend the tree.

For the station of intellect a child must become an old man; in the station of love you see an old man become youthful.

Shams-e Tabrīzī, whoever has chosen to be lowly in love for you, thereby rises to heights sublime as your love.

242

Sāqī, now that you are drunk, fling yourself on me; to recollect tomorrow is credit—smite the neck of credit.

The year is our year, and the ascendant is the ascendant of Venus and the moon; O heart, this pleasure and joy has no bounds—be at rest.

Glow and gaiety have penetrated to the heart of stone and steel; if you do not believe, strike the stone upon the steel.

Look at the host, see the happiness upon his face; sit at this table and dip your bowl in the oil.[84]

Summon up nimble reason and seat it beside happiness; jovially apply your bright soul to bright wine.

The branches are drunk and dancing in the wind of spring; jasmine, be drunk, and cypress, stroke the lily.

They have cut green garments at the shop of the unseen; tailor, rise up, sit at your shop, stick in your needle.

243

What light is that in the midst of the darkness of your soul? A royal splendor is shining in my heart—who is that?

It sppears that it is the fantasy of the king's moonlike face, that it is the succoring shelter of the day of misery.

All this splendor and beauty and grace and loveliness and charm is the Prior of Souls, Shams-e Ḥaqq-e Dīn-e Tabrīzī.

The human soul cannot endure the clear apparition of his qualities; all that it can endure of his qualities, my heart, is by allusion.

For how should eternal qualities display themselves in mortality to a mixture which itself is of the mortal world?

How far does that beauty, which God engraved of His own hand, transcend an image created by Āzar or Mānī![85]

The eye that has beheld him, and then looked on another than him, must be stoned, for it is worthless.

O heart, in loverhood abandon your good name, for the beginning of love is notoriety and evil fame.

In the sea of his love the soul's clothes are an embarrassment; to seek in love for name and bread is rawness, my heart.

Even the love of the generality of people has this specialty, my heart; all the more especially this love which belongs to that lofty assembly.

Zephyr, bring the earth of Tabriz as a present for my sake, for in preciousness it compares with a jewel of the quarry.

244

Lover, open your two eyes and behold in yourself four streams —a stream of water, a stream of wine, streams of milk and honey.[86]

Lover, look into yourself, do not be a laughingstock of men, so that So-and-so says this, and So-and-so says that.

I am the slave of that all-seeing rose which is indifferent whether So-and-so calls it thorn, or So-and-so calls it jasmine.

Then open your eyes henceforward, walk not with the eyes of men, that So-and-so says you are a Guebre and So-and-so a man of true religion.[87]

God of his generosity gave you the eye of vision, to whose languidness the pinion of Gabriel prostrates.[88]

Bandage not the narcissus-eye, and take not the vulture-eye; bandage not the first eye, and look not with the squint-eye.

Lovers of fire have fallen into fire, like the fly which falls from honey into a vat of whey.

Rejoice, you who play at love with the eternal Almighty; with such wings, why should you sorrow over water and clay?[89]

If you desire that Gabriel should become your slave, be gone; prostrate before Adam at once, accursed *dīv*!

If the blood-drinking desert had knowledge of my Kaaba, on all sides a rose bower would appear, on all sides springwater.

You who continue to regard the evil and good of people, how is it you have become content with that? May the Lord help you!

Since heaven itself had not the strength to bear God's trust, how is it that Shams-e Tabrīzī has diffused it in the earth?[90]

245

By God, I have no inclination towards either fat or sweet, nor for the purse full of gold, neither for the golden cup.

You draw the people of earth to heaven; the moon exclaims, "What grace and generosity! What amazing power and authority!"

When your fantasy shines on me like the moon at the full, Venus and the Pleiades bite their forearms and fingers in envy.

Ha, thanks be to God that I have attained this kingdom; it was all true, what your love said to me again and again of old.

When he saw me on tiptoe, he signaled to me saying, "What you desire has come to pass; ho, be secure and be seated!"

All creatures and intoxication of joy bow down before him; lamb and wolf are friendly together, no envy or hatred in the heart;

They are so drunk they cannot tell the way to town from the way home; they know not "whether we are men, extraordinary, or colored clay."

Goblet in hand and distraught, I wonder what am I to do with this? Drink it or bestow it? You tell me, sweet king!

"You drink; what bestowing should there be? For your turn has come." Lo, I have drunk; lo, I have drunk, since I am specified before you.

"Drink this wine of the throne, whereof if you were to place one cup in the hand of a dead man, he would respond to the prompting."[91]

246

Beautiful one, by your roguish eye, signal with your eye; for one moment repair with a glance this your ruin.

Heart and soul, martyrs to your love, in the tomb of the body— pass along by the tomb of those martyrs, pay a pilgrimage.

You are come like a Joseph, all Egypt has cut its hands; display your charm and take my heart and soul, do a deal![92]

Or if you have stamped your foot tyrannically and sworn a vow, then break your vow—what matter? Do expiation.

Say not, "What profit shall I have from this offering of yours?"

You need not profit; give, and take a loss!

Convert this saffronlike cheek into the like of roses and anemones; make a rejoicing heart out of three or four drops of blood.

Since fortune is your slave, it will never rebel against you; king, be an ambassador between us and fortune.

Since sins are as a straw before the mountain of your clemency, look with disdain upon our mountain of sins.

Our body was two drops of blood that became pure and human; you also cleanse the impure quality.[93]

Since souls here become the prisoner of water and clay from the world of the spirit, deliver them from the clay, Abode of War, and make a raid![94]

Since I have repented of words, for the sake of the disciples instead of words issue a meaningful signal and command.

This firelike breath is for the sake of making warm; make a glow other than your breath a source of heat.

You who are King Shams-e Dīn, by the shining manifestation of yourself, make lovely Tabriz the abode of vision.

247

Since you deserted me death is for me joy and ease; without you, death has become for me like honey and milk.

The waterless fish quivers on that rough sand until its feeble soul may become parted from its body.

For the living ones, the water of life has become the water of bitterness; pure sugar has become worse for them than the grave and winding-sheet.

It is no mere game, the drawing of the part to the origin, the All; how often the prophet wept for love of his homeland![95]

The child who does not know his homeland and birthplace desires a nurse; Istanbul or Yemen—they are all one to him.

The star goes to graze in the pasture of the skies; the animal worships earth, like cypress and jasmine.

Though I close my mouth to silence this lamentation, it is not possible to close one's mouth in the belly of the water.

The frog's breath is of water, not of the wind of the air; this is the custom and craft of sea creatures.

Gnostics who are hidden in that ocean of light, their breath is all of darkness-shattering light.[96]

When I reached this point, my pen and tablet broke; the mountain is shattered when it becomes aware of the Lord of Grace.[97]

248

All have eaten and fallen asleep, and the house has become empty; it is time for us to saunter forth to the garden,

To draw the skirt of the apple towards the peach, to carry a few words from the dewy rose to the jasmine.

Springtide is like the Messiah, it is an art, a spell, that the plant-martyrs may arise from their winding-sheets.

Since those fair idols opened their mouths in gratitude, the soul not attaining a kiss is drunk with the perfume of their mouths.

The glow on the cheeks of rose and tulip informs me that there is a lamp hidden in this place under the screen.

The leaf trembles on the twig, and my heart is trembling; the leaf trembles in the wind, my heart for the beauty of Ḳotan.[98]

The hand of the zephyr has fanned the censor till it taught good manners to the children of the garden.

The breath of the Holy Spirit has encountered the trees of Mary; see how husband and wife are playing with hands together [in joy].

The cloud, seeing the lovely ones beneath the canopy, scattered over them jewels and pearls of Aden.[99]

Now that the red rose in joy has rent its skirt, the time has come for the shirt to reach Jacob.[100]

Since the Yemeni carnelian of the Beloved's lips laughed, the scent of God reaches Mohammad from Yemen.

We have spoken much at random, and our heart has not found repose save upon that scattered tress of the King of the time.

249

Wherever you set your foot, my darling, tulip and violet and jasmine spring up.

You breathe upon a piece of clay, and it becomes either a dove or a kite.

You wash your hands in a dish and from the water of your hand that basin becomes of gold.

You recite the *Fāteha* over a grave and a Bu'l-Fotūḥ raises his head from the winding-sheet.[101]

Your skirt strikes against the clutch of a thorn, and its clutch becomes a strumming lute.

Every idol you have broken, O Abraham, receives life and finds intellect from that breaking.

Since the new moon shone upon an evil-starred one, it became the greatest good fortune and he escaped from misfortune.

Every moment there springs from the court of your breast a newborn without mother or father, like Adam.

And thereafter from his side and loins children abound in the earth.

I wanted to speak fifty couplets on this rhyme; I closed my lips, that you might open your mouth.

250

Hear the wordless subtleties, and understand what catches not the understanding.

Inside the stonelike heart of man is a fire which burns up the veil, root and branch;[102]

When the veil is burnt he discovers all the stories of Khidr and *the knowledge from us.*[103]

Between the soul and the heart appears new and ever new forms from the ancient love.

When you recite *By the sun* behold the sun! Behold the mine of gold when you recite *Lam yakon.*[104]

251

Last night I saw Poverty in a dream, I became beside myself from its beauty.[105]

From the loveliness and perfection of the grace of poverty I was dumbfounded until dawn.

I saw poverty like a mine of ruby, so that through its hue I became clothed in silk.

I heard the clamorous rapture of lovers, I heard the cry of "Drink now, drink!"

I saw a ring all drunken with poverty; I saw its ring in my own ear.[106]

From the midst of my soul a hundred surgings rose when I beheld the surging of the sea.

Heaven uttered a hundred thousand cries; I am the slave of such a leader.

252

Though long enough I have sat in fire up to my neck, now I am up to my neck in the water of union with the Beloved.

I said, "I am immersed in your graces up to my neck." The Darling was not content with me up to the neck.

He said, "Make your head a foot, descend into the depths of love, for this affair does not come out right only up to the neck."

I said, "My head, Beloved, is your shoe; only be content, my two eyes, with up to my neck this time."

He said, "You are less than a thorn which was up to the neck in earth for nine months waiting for the rose."

I said, "What is the thorn? For the sake of your rosebed I have sat often in blood up to my neck like the rose."

He said, "Through love you have escaped from the world of allurement, where you were struggling impotently up to your neck.

"You escaped from the world, but not from yourself; your self-existence is a disgrace, and this disgrace is up to your neck.

"Lay not traps cunningly, give up trickery; the trickmaster remains in his own trap up to the neck.

"The trap of this world is a trap through which kings and lions have remained like dogs in the carrion up to the neck.

"There is a stranger trap than this, through which you may see the reasonless fallen up to the ankle, the prudent up to the neck."

Enough of speech, now that breath is cut off; after all, speech does not reach up to the neck from choking.

253

Go, lay your head on the pillow, let me alone; leave me ruined and night-faring and afflicted as I am.[107]

I am writhing with the wave of passion alone through night till day; if you will, care and have mercy; if you will, go and be cruel.

Flee from me that you too may not fall into calamity; choose the path of safety, leave the path of calamity.

We with our tears flowing have crept in the corner of grief; turn the mill a hundred times upon our tears.

A tyrant we have who has a heart like flint; he slays, and no one says to him, "Prepare to pay the blood-money."

To the king of the lovely ones faithfulness is not obligatory; pale lover, you endure, be faithful.

This is a pain of which no cure exists but to die, so how shall I say, "Cure this pain?"

Last night in a dream I saw an elder in the garden of love: he beckoned to me with his hand, saying, "Set out towards me."

If a dragon is on the path, love is like an emerald; with the flash of this emerald repel the dragon.[108]

Enough, for I am beside myself, if you would be a man of superior learning, recite the history of Bū ʿAlī, and admonish Buʾl-ʿAlā.[109]

254

Did you see what January said? Lay brushwood like a stock: if December brought not cold, the cold of both be on me.

Since the cold has become stubborn, lay brushwood on the fire. Do you spare brushwood? Is brushwood better, or the body?

Brushwood is the fainting form, God's love is the fire: burn up the forms, O pure-skirted soul!

Until you burn up the form, your spirit will be frozen, like idol worshipers far from springtime and security.

In firelike love, be happy like silver; since you are a child of Abraham, fire is your dwelling.[110]

By God's command, fire becomes for true men tulip and rose, clusters of basil, willow and lily.

The believer knows the spell and recites it over the fire; the heat remains in it no more, it remains shining as the moon.

Blessed be the spell through which peace befalls in a fire which can transform iron into needle.

The moth flings itself upon the kindled fire because the fire reveals itself lit in the shape of a window.

To Ḥamza arrow and spear appear as scattering roses; in a scatter of roses no man clothes himself in armor.[111]

Pharaoh was dissolved in the water like whey; Moses got on the brow of the water like oil.

Horses of spirit are the carriers of princes; dull and sluggish horses carry packs and dung.

Speech is like a hopper on the mill of meaning; the mill turns by water, not by regulating the hopper.

From that hopper, my brother, the wheat leaps from the bucket and falls in the mill and becomes well and truly ground.

So from that hopper of expression, out of the bucket of greed and negligence, you fall into the mill, that is in a clearly expressed way.

My soul, I am becoming hot, but not from chatter; it is from the golden Sun of the Faith, from whom Tabriz is like a mine.

255

Sit with lovers, altogether choose loverhood; be not for a moment companion with him who is not a lover.

And if it be that the Beloved has drawn the curtain of all might, go, gaze on the face of him who is not veiled;

Behold that face on whose cheeks are the marks of His face; contemplate him on whose brow shines the sun.

Inasmuch as the sun has laid his two cheeks on his cheeks, through his cheeks the moon on earth is checkmated.

In his tresses is the copy of *Thee we serve;* in his eyes the glance *in Thee we beg for succor.*[112]

His body, like the body of a phantom, is without blood and veins; inside and outside it is all milk and honey.

Inasmuch as the Beautiful takes him into his embrace, he has carried away the scent of the Beloved and let go the scent of clay.

He is a morn without a dawn, an evening without henna, an

essence without attributes, a life without sorrow.[113]

How should the sun borrow light from the sky? How should the rosebush borrow perfume from the jasmine?

Be speechless as a fish and pure as the water of the sea that you may quickly become the trustee over the treasury of the pearl.

I will speak in your ear; do not tell anyone. Who is all that? Shams-e Dīn, the pride of Tabriz.

256

I have heard that you are intending to journey; do not. That you give your love to another friend and companion; do not.

You are a stranger in the world; why do you estrange yourself? What heart-wounded victim are you aiming at? Do not.[114]

Do not steal yourself from us, do not go to strangers. You are steathily glancing at the others; do not.

Moon for whom the heavens are topsy-turvy, you waste us and turn us topsy-turvy; do not.

What promise do you make and what oath do you swear? You make a shield of oaths and blandishments; do not.

Where are the pledge and compact you made to your servant? You depart from your pledge and word; do not.

You whose court is higher than being and not being, you are transgressing the bound of being; do not.

You at whose command hell and heaven are slaves, you make paradise like Gehenna to me; do not.

In your sugarcane plot we are secure from poison; you are commingling that poison with the sugar; do not.

My soul is like a fiery furnace; is that not enough for you? Through absence you are making my face pale as gold; do not.

When you withdraw your face, the moon is darkened with grief; you are intending the eclipse of the moon's orb; do not.

Our lips become dry when you bring a draft: why are you wetting my eyes with tears? Do not.

Since you cannot endure the shackling of lovers, why then do you dazzle the eye of reason? Do not.

You do not give sweetmeats to one sick of a fever; you hurt still more him whose sickness you are; do not.

My lawless eye is the thief of your beauty. Beloved, you requite the thievish eye; do not.

Withdraw, comrade, for it is no time for speech. Why do you thrust yourself forward in the bewilderment of love? Do not.[115]

257

Give yourself a kiss, silvery-bodied idol; you who are in Cathay, do not search for yourself in Kotan.

If you would draw a silvery-bodied one into your bosom, where is the like of you? You must kiss the Beloved, then caress your own mouth.

For the sake of your beauty are the robes of the houris; the beauty of every man or woman is the reflection of your lovely face.

The veil over your beauty is the tresses of your hair, else the light of you would have shone out, O sweet of chin.

The painter of the body came towards the idols of the thoughts; his hand and heart were broken, his mouth stood open.

This painted cage is the veil of the bird of the heart; you have not recognized the heart because of the heart-breaking cage.

The heart flung off the veil from the clay of Adam, and all of the angels prostrated themselves.

The intermediary would vanish if only for a moment love's Turk sat down before his grace, saying, "O Chelebi, who are you?"[116]

The eye would be endowed with sight of the unseen, if the glance of Shams-e Dīn, Pride of all of Tabriz, stole a wink at you.

258

Whatever you do, know it is done by Me; whatever the body does, the Soul has done it.

You are my eyes, you are my ears; I have mentioned these two, remember the rest.

If that treasure was not in the world, then to what end would it be a ruined house?

Seek the treasure, my father; move your hand, move your hand.

His sweet scent has become our guide to rose and basil, to rose and basil.

Atom by atom all are purchasers; beware, do not sell your pearl cheaply.

The mouse will come out, the cat will come out, if you open the mouth of the bag.

When love is there, the soul suffers no diminution; may the shadow of the Beloved not be afar!

You will recite the rest of this, moonfaced moon, shining Venus!

259

By your own life I implore, do not withdraw from this heartless wretch; suffer me still, do not make for your house.

Do not think of pretexts, leave excuses aside; treat me not aloofly, be not haughty.

Wine is at hand, fortune our boon companion, and you the *sāqī;* give the wine, play not *sāqī's* frauds.

Cast your glance at your companions who are drunk with you, do not gaze at window and porch and threshold.

Pass not your time save in the lovers' circle, make not your nest save in the tavern quarter.

See, the world is a snare and desire the bait; hasten not into its snare, desire not the bait.

When you have passed out of its snare, set your foot on the sky; let naught but the sphere of the threshold be under your feet.

Heed not sunshine and moonshine; be alone, and seek only that Alone.

Rest not without Him, like a bowl tossed on the water; do not take the bowl and set it running to every kitchen.

Time is bright and dark, warm and cold in turns; make not your abode save at the fountainhead of time.

Praise him not, neither cover him with reproaches; offer not pastries, and do not throw forward that garlic.

But what is the use? For such are the ways of vain idols. Do not say to the brand of fire, "Do not make a flame."

Say to whatever your burn, "Burn," save with separation; that is not allowable, do not perpetuate this one tyranny either.

260

If my words were not worthy of your lips, then pick up a heavy stone and shatter my mouth.

When a child speaks nonsense, does not the loving mother prick his lips to teach him manners?

For the sake of the majesty of your lips, burn and tear and rend and dash to pieces two hundred mouths and worlds.

When a thirsty man boldly runs to the seashore, does not the wave lift up its sword to his neck?

I am the slave of the lily which, having seen your rose bower and been put to shame by your narcissus, its ten tongues became dumb.

But I am like a tambourine; when you strike your hand on me I cry out.

Lay me not aside until the concert grows hot; draw your skirt aside from the impure world.

Yes, the eyes are intoxicated from the rose bower of meaning, yet the song of the bolbol is sweet in the rose bower.

If Joseph's beauty is fairer naked, yet the eyes are not opened save by his shirt.

Though the glitter of the sun of the soul is the origin, no man has reached that heaven without a body.

Silence! for if the corpse-washer binds my mouth, you will hear this melody from the grave after I am dead.

261

O seven seas, bestrew pearls and transmute these things of brass;

O candle of drunkards and cypress of the garden, how long these tricks? At least keep faith.

Every granite rock wept for us, Beloved; cure this our pain.

You angrily turned away your face; for a moment have done with this behavior.

You once showed much beneficence and humanity; redouble that humanity.

Fair of course, O moon and star, be generous in the darkness of night like the moon.

Separate from us the ancient pain, the anguish of sickness, and the orphan's dust.

Though I be in paradise, in gold and silver, without you I am an orphan; cure me.

I have closed my lips and sat in sorrow; open my hand, make for encounter.

262

My darling came to me; through him my roof and door sprang to life.

I said, "Tonight you are my guest, O my provocation and disturbance."

He said, "Let me go; there is important business for me in the city, soul and head of mine."

I said, "By God, if you depart, tonight this bodily form of mine will not live."

"Why, will you not for one night show compassion upon my golden pale cheek?

"Will not your happy eye show compassion upon this languid and wet eye of mine?

"Let the rosebed of your cheek scatter roses over my tears sweet as Kowṣar."[117]

He said, "What can I do, seeing that Fate has poured the blood of all men into my cup?"

I am of Mars, and only blood is in my ascendant, my star.

No incense is accepted by God until it enters my crucible.

I said, "Since your aim is my life, only blood should be my food and dessert.

"You are cypress and rose, I am your shadow; I am slain by you, you are my Ḥaydar."[118]

He said, "Only a rarity shall be my sacrificial offering, O servant of mine.

"Gorjīs is arriving, for every moment he is newly slain in my land.[119]

"Isaac the prophet should have been sacrificed to the dust of my door.

"I am love, and if I shed your blood I will bring you to life in my resurrection.

"Beware, do not flutter in my clutch, do not shrink from my dagger;

"Make not a worry face at death that my breast may give thanks to you.

"Laugh like the rose when Death plucks you out and plunges you in my sugar.

"You are Isaac and I am your father; how should I shatter you, my jewel?

"Love is the father, the lover his flock; of him is born my pomp and pride."

So saying, he departed like the zephyr; the tears flowed from my eyes.

I said, "What would it be to you if you were to be kind and depart slowly, my master?

"Do not hasten: a little more slowly! Life and world and hundred-petaled [rose] of mine.

"No one ever saw me hurry; this is my more lazy pace.

"Yon sphere of heaven, if it tried its utmost, would never reach to where I pass."

He said, "Silence! for this gray horse of heaven goes lamely in my presence.

"Silence! for if you are silent, this flame of mine will fall upon the thicket.

"Do not say the rest of it till another day, that my heart may not flee from my breast."

263

My *sāqī* rises without my speaking and brings that wine of abundant price.

There is no need for me to say, "Bring," he hears the voice of my heart without mouth.

This imprecation is his own grace, his boundless generosity and goodness.

The moon rises, do not say to it, "Arise"; it casts light on you, do not say, "Cast."

O you in time of festivity, the best joy and pleasure and in time of battle, the greatest breaker of ranks.

Excellent guide for all who have lost the way, fine rope for all imprisoned in the well;

The world is like night, and you the moon; you are like a candle, the souls a sconce.

The soul is restless like a mote; with you it becomes tranquil, O excellent tranquillity.[120]

264

You are my life, you are my life, my life; you are my own, you are my own, my own.

You are my king, worthy of my passion; you are my candy, worthy of my teeth.

You are my light; dwell within these eyes of mine, O my eyes and fountain of life!

When the rose beheld you, it said to the lily, "My cypress tree came to my rose garden."

Say, how are you in respect to two scattered things! your hair, and my distracted state?

The rope of your hair is my shackle, the well of your chin is my prison.

Where are you going, drunk, shaking your hands? Come to me, my laughing rose!

265

A cry went up from my tavern, the heavens were split by my litany:

Finally victory has arrived, the Beloved has entered to tend me.

Lord, lord, how He is aching, my unequaled Beloved, to recompense me!

That philosophers' stone makes obedience and faith from my neglect and unbelief and sins.

After my shortcomings He bestows a palace, after my slips He bestows victuals.

He causes the heart of sea and mountain to surge from the heat of the day of my encounter.

If the thoughts of man were not a veil, they would be burnt to ashes by my thoughts.

My drum and flag, my cry and shouting would strike agitation in the army of the spirit;

The fire of my tryst at midnight would strike flames into the horizon of the sky.

266

Come nearer, my pretty idol, my sympathetic idol of like hue with me.

See how my heart has become constricted with your coquettishness, till you say to me, "O my suffering one!"

I battle with my heart as with an enemy till you say, "Bravo, my general!"

How long will you ask, "Why is this face of yours pale?" It is through grieving for you, my rose-hued idol.

Last night all night to Venus reached the lamenting of this lyre-shaped body of mine.

Purchase back my soul from my body, that my soul may escape my shame.

Through the grace of your ruby lips my stonelike heart has become a banker of gold.

Accord peace to my soul and to me, for all my war is on your account.

My foot becomes swifter going than the wind, if you say, "Come, my lame one!"

For this reason I am bound and suspended from you, that my rope [of grapes] through you may become like sugar.

You are indifferent to me, and I am miserable; oh, what shall I become if you desire me?

The Zangī of grief is at the door of happiness of Rūm; ransom my Rūm from my Zang.

I fear not the untimeliness and the distance of the way; through you my parsang has become half a foot.

My old age has become better than childhood, my wrinkled face has become fresh again.

Be silent, be bewildered as silent ones, so that he may say to you, "My silent and bewildered one!"

267

Once more our [crescent] moon has reaped a harvest, and we have paraded forth despite the foe.

Once more the sun has entered Aries, made the world to look like a rose garden.

The blossoms have mirthfully opened their lips, the lily has slily become a tongue.

What satins they have put on in the garden for that tailor who has no scissors or needle!

Every tree has set on its head a tray full of sweetmeats without syrup and oil.

We have made our bellies a drum once more, since the drummer of spring began drumming.

The surface of the water, which in winter was as iron, has become ruffled like chainmail by the wind;

Perchance the early spring is the David of time, who has fashioned a coat of armor out of that iron.[121]

God proclaimed in nonexistence, "Ho, herbs: Those cold ones have left the dwelling.

"Turn your faces to the height of existence like the birds of Abraham from their nest."[122]

That gnostic crane has returned from exile, about him the stammering birds uttering praises.

The routed ones who had become hidden have each put their head out of the window.

The greenclads have put forth their heads, ear and neck full of collars and jewels.

It is concert, and thousands of houris in the garden are stamping their feet on the tomb of January.

Ho, willow, awake and move your head and ears, if you have bright eyes like the narcissus.

I say to speech, "Abandon me"; speech is contentious, it is coming after me.

I do not desire, because of his hard face, to declare the talk of lovers.

The rose calls, "Ye Midianite, rejoice with us whoever was sorrowful."[123]

The earth has become verdant with light, and God has said to the naked, "Adorn yourself."

The fugitives have returned to life, the *dīvān* of the resurrection is now organized.

By God's command they died, then they came to life. He made them decay for a while, then made them fair.

God's sun is rising with bounty, the proof of His handiwork is established.

We have dyed the plants without a dye, we measure their size without a mold.

Paradise on paradise on paradise—dazzles one, take up your home therein.

We have stirred up the souls to the heights; this one has attained union, that one played the Pharaoh.

Ah, be silent and address them with silence, for silence is more revealing of secrets.

268

Lovers, lovers, whoever sees His face, his reason becomes distraught, his habit confounded.

He becomes a seeker of the Beloved, his shop is ruined, he runs headlong like water in his river.

He becomes in love like Majnūn, head spinning like the sky; whoever is sick like this, his remedy is unobtainable.

The angels prostrate before him who became God's dust, the Turk of heaven becomes the servant of him who has become His Hindu [slave].[124]

His love places the aching heart on his hand and smells it; how did not that rejoice which has become His.

Many a breast He has wounded, many a sleep He has barred; that magical glance of His has bound the hand of the magicians.

Kings are all His beggars, beauties clippings of His [beauty], lions drop their tail on the earth before His street-dogs.

Glance once at heaven, at the fortress of the spiritual ones, so many lamps and torches on His towers and battlements.

The keeper of His fortress is Universal Reason, that king without drum and tabor; he alone climbs that fortress who no longer possesses his own ownness.

Moon, have you seen His face and stolen beauty from Him? Night, have you seen His hair? No, no, not one hair of Him.

This night wears black as a sign of mourning, like a black-robed widow whose husband has gone into the earth.

Night makes a pretense and imposture; secretly it makes merry, its eye closes no eye, its brow is set awry.

Night, I do not believe this lamenting of yours; you are running like a ball before the mallet of fate.

He who is struck by His mallet carries the ball of happiness, he runs headlong like the heart about His street.

Our cheeks are like saffron through love of His tulip bed, our heart is sunk like a comb in His hair.

Where is love's back? Love is all face, back and face belong to this side, His side is only face.

He is free of form, His business is all form-fashioning. O heart, you will never transcend form because you are not single with Him.

The heart of every pure man knows the voice of the heart from the voice of clay; this is the roaring of a lion in the form of His deer.

What is woven by the hand of the One becomes revealed, becomes revealed from the workmanship of the weaver and his hand and shuttle.

O souls His shuttle, O our qibla His street, heaven is the sweeper of this street, this earth its mistress.[125]

My heart is burning with envy for Him, my eyes have become His water bags: how should He be wet with tears, while the sea is up to His knees?

This love has become my guest, struck a blow against my soul; a hundred compassions and a hundred blessings to his hand and arm!

I flung away hand and foot and had done with searching; my searching is dead before His searching.

Often I said, "O heart, be silent to this heart's passion"; my *hā* is useless when my heart hears His *hū*.[126]

269

The glow of the light of daybreak is in your emerald vault, the goblet of the blood of twilight is your blood-measuring bowl.

Mile on mile, torrent on torrent come dancing and gliding to the shore of your sea.

With all the abstention and aspiration of the moon, the cap falls off the head of the moon when the moon raises its face to gaze upon your height.

Every morn the nightingales lament like the heart-forlorn ones to the melodies of those attaining your verdant meadow.

The spirits seek vision, the hearts all seek the Beloved; you in whose broad orchard four streams are let flow—one stream pure water, another honey, the third fresh milk, the fourth your ruby wine.[127]

You never give me a chance, you are giving wine upon wine; where is the head, that I may describe the drinking-cup of your wine?[128]

Yet who am I? Heaven itself in the round of this heavy bumper finds not a moment's peace from your love and the craving for you.

Moon of silver girdle, you have experience of love; heaven, loverhood is apparent in your features.

When love is yoked to the heart it wearies of the heart's chatter: heart, be silent! How long this striving and inquiring of yours?

The heart said, "I am His reed pipe, I wail as the breath in me." I said, "Be lamenting now, the slave of whose passion is the soul."

We have opened your door; do not desert your companions; in thankfulness for an all-embracing love which has seized you from head to toe.

270

When laughter leaps full from me, I keep laughter hidden from him; I make a sour face at him; I shout and scream at him.

If you joke and laugh at the sour ones, war arises; I have hidden my laughter, I drop tears at him.

A huge city is my body, grief on one side, I on the other; one side I have water from him, on the other fire.

With his sours I am sour, with his sugars I am sugar; he is my face, he is my back, through him I scratched the back of joy.

A hundred the likes of me and you have become drunk in his meadow, dancing, hand-clapping on the summit of every dome through him.

I am the parrot of candy and sugar, I eat only sugar; whatever sour is in the world, I am far and indifferent to it.

If he has given you sourness, to me he has given honey and sugar; he has made you jolting and lame, me smooth and even of pace.

Whoever travels not on this road, his path is all gully and steep; I who am on this royal road am on a level path through him.

My heart is the *Masjed-e Aqsā*, my heart is the Paradise home; all my traces through him have become houris and light.[129]

To whomsoever God gives laughter, laughter leaps from his mouth; if you doubt Him, I am altogether in acknowledgement of Him.

The rose's portion is laughter, it has no weeping; what shall it do? Lilies and roses are blossoming in my conscious heart through Him.

Patience was saying, "I bear good tidings of union from Him; gratitude was saying, "I am the owner of stocks through Him."

Reason was saying, "I am abstinent and sick through Him"; Love was saying "I am a magician and cutpurse through Him."

Spirit was saying, "I am a pearl-possessing treasure through Him"; Treasure was saying, "I am at the foundation of the wall through Him."

Ignorance was saying, "I am without knowledge and consciousness through Him"; Knowledge was saying, "I am the chief of the *bazar* through Him."

Abstinence was saying, "I understand the secrets through Him"; Poverty was saying, "I am without heart and turban through Him."

If Shams-e Ḥaqq returns to me from Tabriz, all my discourses will be expanded and revealed through Him.

271

Whatever comes of the world's affairs, how does that affect your business? If the two worlds have become an idol-temple, where is that roguish idol of yours?

Grant that the world is in famine, there is no bowl [of wine] and bread any more; O king of the manifest and hidden, where are your measure and store?

Grant that the world is all thorn, scorpion and snake; O joy and gladness of the soul, where are your rose bower and rosebed?

Grant that liberality itself is dead, that miserliness has slain all; O our heart and eye, where are your pension and robe of honor?

Grant that both the sun and the moon have sunk into hell; O succor of hearing and sight, where are your torch and light?

Grant that the jeweler is not after any customer, how shall you not take the leadership? Where is your pearl-raining cloud?

Grant there is no mouth, there is no speech of tongue to tell the secrets; where is the surging of your heart?

Come, leave all this, for we are drunk with union and encounter; the hour is late—come quickly, where is this house of your vintner?

Drunken sharp-glancer of mine, my fellow in heart and hand, if you are not dissolute and in dotage, where are your cloak and turban?[130]

A whore has carried off your cap, another your gown; your face is pale with a moonlike beauty; where is your support and protection?

A stranger is waylaying the path to the drunkards of eternity: why do you not act the policeman? Where is your wound thrust? Where are your gallows?

Silence, word-scatterer! Interpret not to ordinary people what is fit only for the ears of the silent ones; where is your ecstasy and speech?[131]

272

Say, how shall a part of the world depart from the world? How shall moisture escape from water, one leap from two?

No fire dies from another fire, my son; O my heart bleeding of love, wash not my blood in blood.

However much I fled, my shadow did not leave me; shadow must be in charge of me, even though I become as the thread of a hair.

Only the sun has the power to drive away shadows, the sun increases and diminishes them; seek this from the sun.

Though for two thousand years you are running in the back of the shadow, in the end you will see that you are behind and the shadow before.

Your sin has become your service, your pain your blessing, your candle your darkness, your bounds seeking and questing.

I would explain this, only it would break the back of your heart; when you break the glass of the heart, repairs are of no avail.

You must have both shadow and light together; listen to me, lay your head down and prostrate yourself before the tree of the fear of God.[132]

When from the tree of His grace wings and feathers sprout for you, be silent as a dove, do not open your mouth for cooing.

When a frog enters water, the snake cannot reach it; the frog croaks and gives information so that the snake knows where he is.

Even though the cunning frog should hiss like a snake, the feeble frog-sound of his betrays the true voice.

If the frog were silent, the snake would be his prey: when it retires into its corner, the barleycorn and grain become a treasure.

When the golden barleycorn has become a treasure, it does not diminish in the earth; the barleycorn of the soul becomes a treasure when it attains the treasure of *Hū*.

Shall I finish these words, or shall I squeeze them again? Yours is the decree; what am I, O gracious king?

273

The rock splits open in yearning to encounter you; the soul beats wing and pinion in the joy of your air.

Fire becomes water, reason is lain waste, my eye becomes the foe of sleep on account of you.

Rending the robe of patience, reason departs out of itself; your love like a dragon devours both men and stones.

Do not bind the departer, do not turn laughter to mocking; be not cruel, for your servant has none to take your place.

When your water departs to the river, how shall my discourse flow well? Sometimes my breath ceases because you are so shy.

What is the food of your love? This roasted liver of mine. What is my ruined heart? The workshop of your fidelity.

The jar is fermenting; who will drink? The harp sings aloud in the description and praise of you.

Love entered by my door and laid a hand on my head, saw that I was without you, and said, "Alas for you!"

I saw a difficult stage, troubled and very complex; I went, and now remain a heart slain by your hand at your feet.

274

Again I am raging. I am in such a state by your soul that every bond you bind, I break, by your soul.

I am like heaven, like the moon, like a candle by your glow; I am all reason, all love, all soul, by your soul.

My joy is of your doing, my hangover of your thorn; whatever side you turn your face, I turn mine, by your soul.

I spoke in error; it is not surprising to speak in error in this state, for this moment I cannot tell cup from wine, by your soul.

I am that madman in bonds who binds the *dīvs*; I, the madman, am a Solomon with the *dīvs*, by your soul.

Whatever form other than love raises up its head from my heart, forthwith I drive it out of the court of my heart, by your soul.

Come, you who have departed, for the thing that departs comes back; neither you are that, by my soul, nor I am that, by your soul.

Disbeliever, do not conceal disbelief in your soul, for I will recite the secret of your destiny, by your soul.

Out of love of Shams-e Tabrīzī, through wakefulness or night-rising, like a spinning mote I am distraught, by your soul.

275

All my six directions, Beloved, are graven with your beauty, you shine in the mirror, since it has been polished by you.

The mirror sees you according to the measure of its breadth; how shall the shapes of your perfection be contained in the mirror?

The sun asked your sun, "When shall I see you?" It replied, "I shall rise in the time of your setting."

You cannot travel freely in this direction, for like a camel your ropes, O reason, have bound your knees.

How is it that reason, whose splendor is not contained in the seven heavens, entered your snare and bag, O love?

This reason became one grain of the harvest of love, and all your feathers and wings became trapped by that grain.

You plunged once into the sea of the life of God, you saw eternal spirit [life], that spirit became your bore.

Of what use is this [reason's] kingship beside the sovereignty of your love? Of what use his pomp beside your pomp and majesty?

See in the world's ears now a hundred golden rings because of the grace of your answering, out of joy of your questioning.

Raw ones who never received refined gold from your hand are happy with your stones and shards instead of gold.

A hundred skies revolve around your earth, a hundred full moons prostrate before your crescent moon.

With you our carnal soul's dog plays foxy tricks, for the lion prostrates before your jackal.

Like day and night, footless we are journeying, O soul, since every moment from heaven arrives your "Come up!"

What shall be our darkness in the presence of your light? What our evil deeds with your beneficence?

By day we revolve about your tree like a shadow, by night till dawn we lament, secure from your wearying.

Yearning for your reproach, Adam came from the high seat of Paradise down to your vestibule.

The heart's sea thunders and boils with your praise, but I have closed my lips, yearning for your discourse.

276

Both aware and untimely he came as my guest; my heart said, "Who has come?" My soul said, "The moonfaced moon."

He entered the house, we all like madmen searching for that moon gone into the midst of the street.

He was crying out from the house, "I am here"; we, heedless of this cry, go crying everywhere.

That drunken nightingale of ours is lamenting in our rose garden, like ringdoves we are flying and shouting, "Where, where?"

At midnight a crowd leaped out saying, "What? The thief has come?" That thief also is saying, "The thief has come"; and he is the thief.

His shout became so mingled with the shout of all others that not a bit of his shouting stands out in this uproar.

And He is with you means He is with you in this search; when you are seeking, seek Him too in the search.[133]

He is nearer to you than you; why go outside? Become like melting snow, wash yourself of yourself.[134]

Through love a tongue grows in the soul like a lily; keep your tongue silent, imitate the trait of the lily.

277

From these depths depart towards heaven; may your soul be happy, journey joyfully.

You have escaped from the city full of fear and trembling; happily become a resident of the Abode of Security.[135]

If the body's image has gone, await the image-maker; if the body is utterly ruined, become all soul.

If your face has become saffron pale through death, become a dweller among tulip beds and Judas trees.

If the doors of repose have been barred to you, come, depart by way of the roof and the ladder.

If you are alone from friends and companions, by the help of God become a *ṣāheb-qerān* [lord of happy circumstance].[136]

If you have been secluded from water and bread, like bread become the food of the souls, and so become!

278

Sweetly parading you go—my soul of soul, go not without me;
life of your friends, enter not the garden without me.

Sky, revolve not without me; moon, shine not without me;
earth travel not without me, and time, go not without me.

With you this world is joyous, and with you that world is joy-
ous; in this world dwell not without me, and to that world depart
not without me.

Vision, know not without me, and tongue, recite not without
me; glance behold not without me, and soul, go not without me.

The night through the moon's light sees its face white; I am
light, you are my moon, go not to heaven without me.

The thorn is secure from the fire in the shelter of the rose's
face: you are the rose, I your thorn; go not into the rose garden
without me.

I run in the curve of your mallet when your eye is with me;
even so gaze upon me, drive not without me, go not without me.

When, joy, you are companion of the king, drink not without
me; when, watchman, you go to the king's roof, go not without
me.

Alas for him who goes on this road without your sign; since
you, O signless one, are my sign, go not without me.

Alas for him who goes on this road without my knowledge;
you are the knowledge of the road for me; O road-knower, go
not without me.

Others call you love, I call you the king of love; O you who are
higher than the imagination of this and that, go not without me.

279

Last night in sleep I dreamed—yet what sleep is there for
lovers?—that I was searching inside the Kaaba for where a
prayer-niche might be.

The Kaaba of the spirits, not that Kaaba which, when you
reach it on a dark night, you say, "Where is candle or moon-
light?"

Nay, rather its foundations are of the light of the whole world,
from which the rays of your spirit take light. Only how can the

soul endure it?

Its hospice is all light, its carpeting is knowledge and reason, its Sufis all bewildered, where is the clatter of the shoes?[137]

Fortunate one, the crown and throne you hold hidden in you are beyond the imagination of Kay-qobād and Sanjar and Sohrāb.[138]

Bird of heart, fly amidst the garden of its beauty, for there is a secure abode; where is snare or beating-stick?

There is a gift in the midst of your body's loans; search in the middle of the soul for the gift of Giver.

In describing from afar the discourse of time became prolix; now that I have reached my tent-tope, where now is prolixity?

Since you quitted the clay, you forthright entered the garden of the heart; so from that side is there naught but concert and pure wine?

Since you left the salt marsh of the body for the garden of the soul, is there naught but rose and basil, tulip and fountains of water?

Since you have seen thousands of beauties that were not of body, why do you say, "Where is the beauty of the Opener of Doors?"

Faqīh, for God's sake, learn the science of love, for after death, where are "lawful," "unlawful" and "obligatory?"[139]

When in time of pain and affliction you quickly find His door, you say once more, "Where is He?" Where is the door of His palace?"

Wait till the wave of union with Him snatches you away and you become unseen, then you may say, "Where is the world of causation?"

If the script of Ebn Bawwāb has become your fancy in calligraphy, read the letter of His love, and it will show you where the Doorkeeper is.[140]

Beware, say not of every man that he is God's deputy; come to the court of the *qāżi*, then see where the deputies are.[141]

Until you box your ears, you will see only men's affairs; when you rub your eyes, you will say, "Where is his light?"

In the tavern of reality, before the destitute drunkards, in such a pure wine you will not see where lees and straw are and secondary causes.

In the mortal reckoning your life has been wasted without

reckoning; behold the purity of the Beloved; where is the similitude of the reckoners?

When the wine makes you brave and you plunge into the sea of the heart, you will strike up this melody: "Where is the bottom of this sea?"

280

Happy the moment which we, you and I, sit in the palace, with two forms and two figures but with one soul, you and I.[142]

The beauty of the garden and the birdsong will confer upon us the water of life at that time when we enter the garden, you and I.

The stars of heaven will come to gaze on us; we shall show them the moon's sickle, you and I.

You and I, unselfed, will be collected together in ecstasy, joyful, and indifferent to idle fable, you and I.

The parrots of heaven will all be sugar-cracking in the place where we laugh in suchwise, you and I.

This is still more amazing, that you and I here in one corner in this very moment are in Iraq and Khorasan, you and I.

In one form upon this earth, and in another form in eternal paradise and the land of sugar, you and I.

281

You who have made the lovers' whole baggage a wager, do not shed the blood of these lovers, and do not depart.

See the traces of blood at the top of the road, hear the bloody cry coming from all sides.

I said to this heart, "See his mallet; if you are a ball, run into this mallet."

The heart said, "In the curve of his mallet I have become old and new a hundred thousand times."

How should the ball of the heart hide from the mallet? For in this desert there is neither well nor ditch.

The cat of the soul is the sneeze of the lion of eternity; the lion trembles when the cat mews.[143]

This is the gold of the mine of Shams-e Tabrīz; search it grain by grain, it is all pure.

282

Sit with your comrades, do not go to sleep; do not go to the bottom of the sea like a fish.

Be surging all night like the sea; no, do not go scattered like a torrent.

Is not the water of life in darkness? Seek in darkness, and do not hurry away.[144]

The nightfarers of heaven are full of light; you too, go not away from the company of your companions.

Is not the wakeful candle in a golden dish? Go not into earth like quicksilver.

The moon shows its face to the night-travelers; be watchful, on the night of moonshine do not go.

283

I went to the master's street and said, "Where is the master?" They said, "The master is a lover and is drunk and wandering from street to street."

I said, "I have a duty, at least you give me a clue; after all, I am the master's friend, not an enemy."

They said, "The master has fallen in love with that garden; seek him in the garden or beside the stream."

Drunkards and lovers go after their beloved; if a man has fallen in love, go and wash your hands from him.

The fish that has known water remains not on land; how should a lover stay in the sphere of color and scent?

The frozen snow that has seen the face of yon sun is devoured by the sun, though it be heap on heap.

Especially he who is in love with our king, a king peerless, faithful, sweet-tempered.

Any copper which that infinite, immeasurable, incomparable alchemy touches becomes gold at the word *Return*.[145]

Sleep away from the world, and flee from the six directions; how long will you foolishly wander and roam hither and thither?

Eventually in the end they will bring you of your own choice, go with glory and honor before the king.

Had there not been a meddler in the midst, Jesus would have

revealed the mystery line by line.[146]

I have closed the road of the mouth and opened the secret way; I have escaped by one cup of wine from the frenzy of speech.

284

I am not satiated, not satiated with your laughing lips; a thousand blessings on your lips and teeth!

Has any man ever wearied, my son, of his soul? You are my soul since my soul and yours are one and the same.

I am thirsty and suffering from dryness, my death and life are from water; pass around the cup, for I am the slave of your turning around.

You make dispensation, go offer me to yourself that my head may raise itself up from your shirt.

Though my two hands are wounded, my hand belongs to you; of what use are my hands without your breath and incantation?

Your love said, "Sir, come into my private chamber, that no thief may make designs on your inner chamber."

I said, "Blessed one, I have become a ring on this door so that no thought of me may trouble your doorkeeper."

He said, "You are both standing at the door and in my bosom, exterior and interior—both homelands are yours.

Silence, and recite no more; sufficient should be this hospitality and table. For all eternity Rūm and Turk shall eat of your table.

285

The light of my heart is your lovely face, my wings and pinions your gentleness;

Festival and *'arafa* are your laughter, my musk and rose age your sweet scent.[147]

My sign is the disc of your moon, my place of shade your lovely hair.

My prostration-place is the dust of your door, my leaping-place your delightful street.

My heart goes not to others, since it has gone in your sweet direction.

Even if my heart goes to others, your sweet "person" will draw it back.

My intoxication is of your being, my plunging-place your sweet river.

I have become like gold from your silvery bosom, I have become single through your sweet fold.

I lay my head; and how should not your sweet ball lay down its head before your mallet?

I will be silent, silent, since my clamoring is shattered by your sweet cry.

286

Come, beat the drum of fidelity, for your hour has come; give wine red as the Judas flowers, for your Judas tree has blossomed.

Let us press new wine from the sweet grapes of your garden, let us scatter fruits from your lusty young tree.

Drive not soul and reason from the table of your bounty; what do two or three flies consume to diminish the plenty of your table?

The desire of all the desirous is but one grain of your harvest; the two worlds are but two small townships in your world.

If all day the sun strikes the sword of light, it becomes less than a mote before your terrible lance.

Since the soul of heaven kisses the earth before you, on what wing shall earth fly towards your heaven?

It sits with broken wings, gazing towards you, for in that same moment there arrives to it the succor of your present.

No night nor dawntide has passed in the world, in which my breath has not been set afire by the threat of your watchman.

Did you not make a promise to me? Did you not swear an oath, that at the time of my going up your ladder should arrive?

When you gaze on your servant with that narcissus eye, his soul flies from the place to your placelessness.

You cherish him saying, "Sorrowful one, do not grieve henceforward, for heaven itself has thundered with your loud lamentation.

"I am more compassionate in cherishing than mother and father; it was to mature you that your trial occurred.

"I will make a garden, a Paradise, a cure out of your pain; out of your smoke I will fashion a new heaven better than this.[148]

"I have spoken all, yet I have not spoken the rest of the matter, Beloved, for it is better that men should hear your secret from your own mouth."

287

Sāqī of the moonface, circulate the cup, deliver me out of shame and name.

Sāqī, I am a prisoner in your snare, for you have laid at every step a snare.

Have done with sloth, seize me! Be not slothful, for the tribe has departed.

Is not sobriety the alighting-place of every care? Is not joy banned in anxiety?

Fast, for fasting is great gain; the faster drinks the wine of the spirit.[149]

It is in tradition that whoever keeps the fast sees the moon of God in the evening time.[150]

It is not just that when I enter by the door, you should flee from me by the roof:

You flee and I crying after you, "Be patient one moment, O fleet of pace!"

Muslims, Muslims, what remedy is there? For I am consumed with fire, and yet this business is unsettled.

There is no remedy but pure wine in cups which noble men have circulated.

The tale of lovers has no end, so we will be satisfied with this, and so farewell!

The answer of Motanabbī's saying is this: 'A heart which wine cannot console.'[151]

288

There are a few dissolutes this side, hidden in the shade of the heart, and yonder sun shines from the roof of the heart upon their souls;

Every star became a Venus, every mote a sun, sun and stars before them spinning like motes.

Reason and heart, gone astray, have carried all the souls to heaven; every one of them has become a Kay-ḵosrow and a king without parasol and standard.[152]

You have slain many a mount and gone around the world; journey into your soul, and behold a people become altogether soul.

With this divine benefaction, with this beauty and loveliness, see the command-worshippers absorbed in the command.

Their hearts are as mirrors, those rancorless hearts of theirs; their hearts like the field of the skies, a king entering the field.

Through their jubilees and ululations, their sugar-cracking lips, dessert and wine and that other thing have become cheap in our town.

If I were unselfed as last night and thought not of the disturbance, unselfed I would have spoken the rest of this;

But for now I close my mouth, because I am in pawn to myself, till the time when my heart has become drunk with him.

King of the kings of the soul, Shams-al-Ḥaqq Tabrīz—through him every soul has become a sea, every body a coral.

289

Lovers, lovers, I am mad; where is the chain? Chain-rattler of the soul, your clamor fills the world.

You have forged another chain and flung it upon my neck; you have galloped from heaven to waylay the caravan.

Rise, soul, from the world, fly from earth and earth's plot; for our sake this torch is revolving in heaven.

He who is pained at heart, how shall his way be barred by rain and mud? That man is quit of love for whom mountain has not become a mustard grain.

One day a hermaphrodite cried, saying, "Wicked shepherd, why, that goat is biting me, he looked at me from the flock."

The shepherd said, "He bites the hermaphrodite and perhaps slays him underfoot, but should that trouble a real man?" "You have spoken well," said the other.

Where is your reason, if you speak? Where your foot to go running, to go from dry land to sea and become secure from the earthquake?

Then you will become king of kings, enter the ternal kingdom, rise higher than the heaven, depart from this dunghill;

Active like the Universal Reason, surging like a sea of honey, like the sun in Aries, like the moon in Virgo.

A hundred crows and owls and doves are making melody in your ears; if only this clamor were less, you would hear the sounds of the heart.

If you are a man of heart, become without heart; if you have reason, become mad, for this partial reason is becoming a stye in the eye of your love,

So that the unseen form may arrive and draw you out of form —for this problem has become difficult through its tangled locks.

But on this road you must trail the skirt of joy because the stage is drenched with lovers' blood.

Go, go, heart, with the caravan; go not alone on the stage because this pregnant age is giving birth to troubles;

There you will be freed from pains, and go in the protection of God; go in the sea like a skiff. Heart, you have gone; go without complaining.

When you have removed heart from soul, you have escaped from war and peace; you have become free and unconcerned with both shop and grain.

Your soul has escaped from anxiety, the road to dangers is barred; he who is attached to you, is always in forty day seclusion.

Since by day you have become secure from this uproarious Rūmī, by night too do not worry about this jangling Zangī.

Be silent, sweet of presence; *sāqī*, bind up your waterskin, because the waves are not contained in pitcher and flagon.

290

Happy-cheeked *sāqī* of mine, give the cup like pomegranate blossom; if for my sake you will not give for the sake of the heart of the Beloved.

Sāqī, you are the darling, you are the sick man's cure; quick, give the draft of gladness and healing to the sick.

Pour wine out in this bowl, smite the neck of anxiety; now, do not break my heart, my heart and sweetheart, and give.

Open that tavern, abandon this rowdiness; give to the thirst-stricken lover from the vintner's vat.

You are the soul of spring and garden, the glory of cypress and jasmine; now make no excuses, roguish idol, but give!

When you set foot on trickery and start away from the drunkards' hands our enemy will rejoice; despite strangers, give!

Give not grief and sighing, open the way only to joy; a sigh proceeds from the wayless; open the way; give audience.

We are all intoxicated of the encounter, athirst for the bumper of immortality; as pawns, give robe and turban before the *sāqī*.

I am athirst of old, hot of heart and breast; break the beaker and cup, give much, without measure.

You are both moon and moonshine, I am the fish of this water; the moon cannot reach the fish, so give generously of the moonshine.

291

I am seeing a moon outside the eye in the eye, which neither eye has seen nor ear heard of.

I do not see tongue and soul and heart save without myself, from that moment that I stole a glance at that cheek.

Had Plato seen the loveliness and beauty of that moon, he would have become even madder and more distressed than I.

Eternity is the mirror of the temporal, the temporal the mirror of pre-eternity—in this mirror those two are twisted together like his tresses.

A cloud beyond the senses whose rain is all spirit; sprinkling on the dust of the body—what rains he has rained!

The moonfaced ones of heaven, seeing the picture of his face, have become ashamed before that beauty and scratched the back of their necks.[153]

Posteternity took the hand of pre-eternity and took it towards the palace of that moon: having seen both, it laughed in jealous pride at the two.

About and around his palace what lions there are, roaring jealously, aiming at the blood of the self-sacrificing, adventurous men.

Suddenly the word jumped from my mouth, "Who is that king? Shams-al-dīn king of Tabriz"; and at those words my blood surged.

292

Undaunted you are coming from my breast into my sight, chanting a potent spell and confused stories.

With one breath you bring into whirling the heavens and firmament; what would one rotting perception be before your spell?

You wash away the sins of both worlds at a single penitence; why have you tightened my slip around your finger?

You have a Job in every corner, a Jacob on every side; love has broken their door and stolen their cloths from the house.

Parade forth to the cemetery and in that garden proclaim, "Rise, ancient dead, dance, crumbled body!"

At once the whole cemetery becomes populated like a city, all dancing, all happy, fate turning back from all.

I do not boast of this at random, I am not weaving a fantasy; I have seen this a hundred ways, I am not speaking of what I have not seen.

If anyone says, "I have fled from the people, I have gone," say, "He speaks the truth if his shirt is torn from behind."[154]

Be silent; listen, speaker, to the sorrow of the beloved with the lover; the effect of the quest is obstinate, so long as the questor is a seeker.

293

Suddenly, having eaten nothing and taken away nothing, I fell from the garden palace and pavilion into the depths of such a well.

The world was no festival for me; I beheld its ugliness, that yellow wanton puts rouge on her face.

How does rouge beautify that thorn of evil root? That thorn which has sunk into every liver and kidney?

She came, that blind crone, with a crown of roses, her black ribbon let loose, having blackened her eyebrows with indigo.

Look not at her anklets, regard her black legs; puppetry is very pretty—when behind a screen!

Go, wash your hands of her, Sufi of well-washed face; shave your heart of her, man of the shaven head!

Unlucky and heavy of soul is he who seeks fortune from her; he is gone in bondage to greatness, and burns like a chip.

Come to our aid, Beloved, amongst the heavy-hearted, you who brought us into this wheel out of nonexistence.

Silence! Speak only of that infinite one of sweet breath; how long will you make discourse of these numbered breaths?

294

O you whose soul had informed my soul of itself, your thought every moment has made an impression on your slave.

Whatever you think whatever enters your mind, that same instant that thing passes into your servant's mind.

My soul has become occupied with your graceful airs; your guile in secret has wrought another thing.

Every morn the reed laments, remembering your lip; your love fills the mouth of the reed with candy and sugar.

Because of your moonlike face and your stature and waist, this soul of mine has made itself like the new moon.

When I make myself like a belt, perhaps you will come to my waist, O you whose eye you have fixed on me in wrath.

In wrath you gazed and turned my head up and down, so that this wandering heart journeyed out of itself.

295

That stranger-beloved of mine has returned to the house; to-day gaze about and behold strange forms!

See the faithful friends, see the brethren of purity, dancing because that treasure has returned to the ruin.[155]

O eye, behold the garden; ear, gather the words, open your sweet lips, beloved of fair legend.

Sāqī, today unthriftily pour the immortal wine; what does the sea diminish through those two or three measures?

Measure and measure in wine is not duality, if you want it to become one, break the two measures.

I am a falcon of the hunt, beloved, do not keep me in bounds; I will be no more like an owl in a ruin.

I am not content with you, patience has strayed from my heart; go, speak to another, I will not listen to your fable.

I am a grain of the skies, for a while I am in this earth; when the justice of spring comes the grain becomes green.

You are the bane of birds; of that grin which you know, you scatter a handful from a garner full of grain.

You who have given me lustre a hundredfold like the blue sky, beloved, answer frankly, is that so or not?

Beloved, once more shake the chain and from afar gaze upon the madmen.

This is the very rose bower of fortune, Lord, what a tree is this! A hundred drunken nightingales every moment make their nest here.

The soul comes, being dragged by the ear; the heart comes to the lovely ones, because spring has come and that stranger December has gone.

296

Every day is festival and Friday for the poor; has not yesterday's Friday become an ancient festival?[156]

O soul, robed in festive garb like the festival moon, made of the light of the beauty of yourself, not of woolen frock;

Like reason and faith sweet outside and inside, not garlic stuffed in the heart of a walnut-sweet.

Put on such a frock and go about in this ring, like the heart clear and bright in the vestibule of the heart.

On a running river, O soul, how shall a straw stand still? How can rancor make its dwelling in the soul and spirit?

In the eye of sanctity these words are a branch new and fresh; in the eye of sensual perception, they are like an ancient legend.

297

O formless Beloved of the pure form-fashioner, O you who have given the cup full of tumult to the lovers,

You have closed your mouth against uttering secrets, and opened in the heart the door which I do not mention.

Since your beauty secretly cast off the veil, heart has gone after saki and hand after wine.

In the morning when your image drove forth riding, holy spirits, as numberless as the sand, followed on foot;

And those who are famous in heaven for their adoration broke their rosaries and pawned their prayer rugs.

They cannot endure to gaze on your face unveiled; your beauty exceeds all that I say.

My soul runs after you like a raging camel; my body is a collar bound upon the neck of that camel.

Shams-al-Ḥaqq Tabrīz, my heart is pregnant by you; when shall I see a child born under your auspices?

298

The dissolutes are all assembled in the Magian monastery; give one bumper to that unique elder.

The blood-shedding master, love, has seized door and roof, and reason is fugitive from house to house.

That most mighty beauty flung aside one veil, and all the people of the time departed out of the veil.

The same is with the lovers who fell into this sea; what place is there for safety and security?

How shall love grow cold from the voice of reproach? A lion never runs from a woman's scream.

Fill the bumper with the divine wine, leave not the "gods" of nature standing in the midst.

First give that bumper to the talkative soul, so that its speaking faculty may not utter any more legends.

Once speech is blocked, a torrent will come so that you will see not one sign left of beings and places.

What a fire Shams-al-Ḥaqq Tabrīz has kindled! Brave, fire, congratulations, O flames!

299

This midnight who has come like moonshine? It is the messenger of love, coming from the prayer-niche.

Bringing a torch, he has set fire to sleep; he has come from the presence of the unsleepy king.

Who is this who has started all this tumult in the city, who came upon the harvest of the darvish like a flood?

Who is this? Say, for in all the world there is none but he, a king came to the door of the house of a doorkeeper.

Who is this who has spread such a table of bounty, who has come laughing, to lead the companions to the table?

A cup is in his hand which makes an end of the dervish; from that grape's juice the color stains his lips.

Hearts are trembling, all souls impatient—one fraction of that trembling has fallen upon quicksilver.

That gentleness and grace with which he treats his servant is the same gentleness and grace which make the ermine.

Of that lament and those tears which are the dry and wet of love, one gentle melody has reached the waterwheel.

A bunch of keys is under love's armpit, come to open all the gates.

Bird of the heart, if the hunter has broken your wings, yet the bird escapes from the snare when it is beaten and broken [dead].

Silence! Embodied similitudes are not mannerly, or manners have never entered your ear.

300

As it is late and raining, to home, to home! Welcome, all friends, to home, to home!

How long like owls banished about the ruins? To home, to home!

Bright-hearted companions, haste, despite all the blond ones, to home, to home!

You reasonable, sober, full of sorrow, do not disturb our hearts! To home, to home!

How long this loveplay with devil's forms, calling them houris? To home, to home!

You have seen the grain and not seen the harvest; even so are ants, to home, to home!

Make not how and why; friend, leave grazing to cattle, to home, to home!

In that house is the concert of the circumcision feast, with the ritually pure, to home, to home!

Shams-al-dīn-e Tabrīz has built a home for the naked; to home, to home.

301

Your heart has become like granite rock, and what can be done with granite rock?

What can glass do with granite rock, except become shattered to pieces.

You laugh like the true dawn that the star may yield its life before you.

Since love opened its bosom, thought has fled into boundary; When patience perceived that flight, it too escaped on horse.

Patience and reason are gone; passion remained, weeping and in a fever.

Some men, being separated from your wine, are fallen on the road like dregs;

Though their livers have turned to blood, yet they are nimble and reckless on this path.

Because of this business we have become strangers to reason and to the busybody heart.

Love is the reality of command; poetry is the drum of indication.[157]

Beware, for our prince is galloping, every morning he is on a raid.

Leave this theme of loneliness and separation, out of terror of which descriptive language breaks.

The imam has fled; *mo'azzen,* be silent, descend from the minaret.

302

What is this hurricane blowing along from heaven? Hundreds of thousands of ships staggering and reeling before it.

The ship escapes through the wind and is sunk by the wind; by the wind it is given life and is done to death.

The wind in God's command is like the breath in yours—by your command brought to cursing or reciting praises.

Know that the winds are various as fanned by the fate of predestination; by the zephyr the world is prosperous, by the pestilence it is reduced to a waste.

Lord, you have shown the wind, do not hide the fan; to see the fan is the lamp of the breast of the pure ones.

Whoever sees it as a secondary cause is surely a form-worshiper; whoever sees it as cause has become the reality-knowing light.

The people of form give their lives for the desire of a bead; to the eyes of people of the sea of reality, pearls have become cheap.

The imitator, becoming the dust of true men, transmits reports from them; the others keep silence, concealed behind them.

The seeker kept his eye to the path and picked up chippings; see that chipping-picker of the road has now entered the mine.

We tremble over our faith as a mother over her child; of what should that clever one tremble who has become entirely faith?

Like a moon you are waning in the desire for leadership; let me see you like a sun, become a king without retinue.

How long will you say that smoke is a proof of fire? Silence! Let me see you become without smoke both fire and proof.

Say how long heaven has turned and goes on turning over your head; let me see you like Messiah gone above heaven!

You who seek a portion from me—"Bring this and that!"—let me see you escape from this and that, and become that and that.

Enough howling drunkard, chattering talker, let me see you become silent-speaking like the pan of the balance.

303

Ha, to and enter the sea; do not look on from afar, for the pearl is in the depths of the sea, the foam on the shore.

When you have seen the face of the king, go forth from the house like a pawn; when you have seen the face of the sun, become lost like a star.

When by that slave-cherishing you have become pure and a man of prayer, invite all like the *mo'azzen* from the minaret.

Gaze on this moon through which your heart has become bright, look upon this king who has arrived on horseback.

I will not fear and tremble when he draws the dagger of omnipotence; by God I will give his dagger a bribe and a portion.

What water is there that matches his grace? For he produces two hundred fountains from the breast of marble and rock.

All day you dance for vermicelli and porridge; what do you know of the desire of the heart for his verse and song?

Since I saw his silvery breast I flee from silver and gold, for his breeze flees away from the hand that counts silver.

You have no fruit because you are light-laden like the willow; you have nothing of that business because you have become a jack-of-all-trades.

All the pilgrims have gone to the sanctuary and seen the Kaaba; you have not even bought a camel with a broken bridle.

Look at your companions, all drunk and dissolute; be silent, and become likewise, you howler.

304

Give that spirited wine, for we are all in such a state that we cannot tell wine from cup, head from foot.

We are all fresher than the lily and the rose branch, become entirely spirit and spirited glow.

All men are in the bond of passion, and passion is our slave, for we have all escaped from this cycle of time.

Like the reed pipe we make voice at the sugar lip of the Beloved; we sell the shop for we are all mine.

The light of the sun devours our bodies like a shadow, for in form we are like being and space.

Our faces are saffron-pale out of fear for the evil eye; we are companions of the garden and tulipbed.

We bring the Qur'an and swear an oath to the *sāqī:* "But from your hand and palm we will not take wine."

Whoever has a soul catches the scent of the rose garden of the soul; whoever has that realizes we are all that.

Our hearts are free of care like the heart of a bird, for we are all lighthearted for that heavy cup.

Kings yield up their crowns of gold in love for our path, for we are more belt-bestowing than youthful fortune.

Seek our souls in the front line of battle, for we go forward like arrow and lance.

We do not sit behind the veil of the shadows of mankind, for like the light of dawn we all tear veils apart.

We were evening, through the sun of the world we have become morning; we were wolves, now we are famous shepherds.

Since Shams-e Tabrīz displayed his soul-adorning cheek, we are running like the spirit towards him with heart and soul.

305

O soul, who is that standing in the house of the heart? Who may be on the royal throne but the king and the prince?[158]

He signaled with his hand, "Tell me, what do you want of me?" What does a drunken man desire but sweetmeats and a cup of wine?

Sweetmeats hanging from the heart, a cup of pure light, an eternal banquet laid in the privacy of "He is the Truth."[159]

How many deceivers there are at the wine-drinkers' feast! Beware, lest you fall, soft and simple man!

In the circle of reprobates beware lest you be eye-shut like the bud, mouth-open like the rose.

The world is like a mirror, the image of the perfection of Love; men, who has ever seen a part greater than the whole?

Go on foot like the grass, for in this rose garden the Beloved like a rose is riding; all the rest are on foot.

He is both sword and swordsman, both slain and slayer, all Reason, and giving reason to the mind.[160]

That king is Ṣalāḥ-al-dīn—may he endure forever, may his bountiful hand be perpetually a necklace on my neck![161]

306

I saw my sweetheart wandering about the house; he had taken a rebec and was playing a melody.

With a plectrum like fire he was playing a sweet melody, drunken and dissolute and charming from the Magian wine.

He was invoking the *sāqī* in the air of Iraq; the wine was his object, the *sāqī* was his excuse.[162]

The moonfaced *sāqī*, pitcher in his hand, entered from a corner and set it in the middle.

He filled the first cup with that flaming wine; did you ever see water sending out flames?

He set it on his hand for the sake of the lovers, then prostrated and kissed the threshold.

My sweetheart seized it from him and quaffed the wine; flames from that wine went running over his face.

He was beholding his own beauty, and saying to the evil eye, "Never has there been, nor shall there come in this age, another like me."

307

I am sprung from you and likewise you have devoured me, I melt in you since through you I froze.

Now you press me in your hand, now under your foot with grief; for the grape does not become wine until it is pressed.

Like the light of the sun, you have cast us on the earth, then little by little carried us back in that direction.

We return from the body's window like light into the orb of a sun, pure of sin and blemish.

Whoever sees that orb says, "He has become alive," and whoever comes to the window says, "So-and-so is dead."

He has veiled our origin in that cup of pain and joy; in the core of origin we are pure, all the rest left behind like dregs.

Source of the source of souls, Shams-e Ḥaqq-e Tabrīz, a hundred livers are on fire for you—so how many kidneys?[163]

308

The sun has risen from the depths of the water, hear *Lā ilāha illa 'llāh* from every mote.[164]

Why speak of motes? When the sun of the soul arrived, they robbed from the sun its very cloak and cap.

The moon of the heart like Adam has emerged from water and clay, and a hundred suns like Joseph are going down into the well.

Lift a head from the earth, for you are not less than an ant; carry to the ants the tidings of the plain and threshing floor.

The ant was satisfied with that rotted grain because it was not aware of our verdant ear of corn.

Say to the ant, "It is springtime, and you have hands and feet; why do you not make your way from the tomb to the open land?"

Why speak of ants? Solomon has rent the robe of yearning; punish me not, O God, for this useless image.

But they cut a gown to fit the purchaser's figure; though the garment is long, the stature is short.

Bring a long stature, that we may cut a gown before whose length the moon's bowstring is broken.

I keep silence hereafter, that through my silence truth and falsehood may be separated as grain from chaff.

309

Since I am intoxicated with your face, learned sage, gaze on me with those intoxicated eyes.

Through your intoxicated eyes my heart writhes (for it is mad); drunkard and madman have a liking for each other's ways.

See my wasted heart and look fondly on me, for the sun gazes fondly upon ruins.

Go gaze, so that, by that one gaze which you gaze, marvelous trees will emerge from a single seed.

Your two eyes are Persian-Turk and drunk and blood-spilling; the Persian shoots Turkish arrows.[165]

They have so plundered me and the house of the heart, that Hasanak is running with naked feet in the house.[166]

We will come into the garden of your face and break up the house; we will manually turn a thousand houses into a desert.

Ṣalāḥ-al-dīn, you are as the moon and have no need of this description, even as the tress-tip of houris needs no comb.

310

For a moment lay your cheek on the cheek of this drunkard, for a moment put behind your war and cruelty.

If it be hard, I bring out silver in my hand; put in this hand wine like gold.

You who have opened the doors of the seven heavens, lay the hand of generosity on my fettered heart.

All I have to offer is not-being; give the nickname of being to my not-being.

You are both breaker and binder of the broken; lay the balm of the soul on my broken head.

Do not put a seal on that sugar and pistachio nut; lay everlasting love upon this servant.

I have told you fifty times, O heart: do not hunt, put your foot in this net.

311

Circumambulating about your moon, the moon and sky and Jupiter, the sun and hooplike sphere come into your sphere—

O lord, am I seeking you or are you seeking me? O my shame! So long as I am, I am one and you are another;

Suspending us and me, shedding the blood of both, raising up something else, neither of man nor peri.

Let foot not remain, for foot carries us to the thorn bush; let head not remain, for the head becomes infidel through two-headedness.

One water flowing amidst the stream, one water frozen on the bank of the stream; the former swift, the latter sluggish; beware, swift one, lest you congeal.

The sun says to the stone, "For this reason I shone on your stone, that you might escape from stoniness and set foot on gemhood."

The sun of eternal love has shone in your heart; first, that your servanthood might increase, and lastly, that you might show mastery.

The sun says to the unripe grape, "I have come to your kitchen so that you may not sell vinegar anymore but make a trade of sweetmaking."

The king says to the falcon, "I bound up your eyes so that you may break with your own kind and only regard my face."

The falcon says, "Yes, I am obedient; only on your beauty I gaze, only by your image I pass, and serve you with my soul."

The rose says to the garden, "I displayed my robes so that you might sell all your wares and make do with me."

He who takes gold from here and makes do with another beloved—sit awry and say truly, what is that from? From assishness?

There is a man who gives up the ass to buy Jesus; it is of assishness that you give up Jesus to buy the ass.

Jesus turns the drunkard into gold, and if he be gold, makes him into a jewel; if a jewel, he makes him better still, better than the moon and Jupiter.

You are not a Jupiter without worth, but the light of *God has purchased:* if you have anything of Joseph, you take the scent of this shirt.[167]

To me, as to Mary, dates come forth from a withered branch without cause; to me, like Jesus, mastership comes unasked in the cradle.

See the grapes without garden and vine, the light without day and night; this glorious fortune, given by God without the process of judgment.

Through my firelike face the world's bath became hot; like children weep less for a picture painted on the bathhouse wall.

Tomorrow you will see its face become food for snake and mouse, those narcissus eyes a gateway of ants.

You are the moonshine driven to the moon, the wall left dark; *to Him we return* has come true—Look yonder, if you can see.[168]

Or go to Tabriz, enjoy Shams-al-dīn, or believe the words of the truthful describers.

312

Beware, Joseph of the fair name, come not on the road without a fellow traveler; break not away from the Jacob of wisdom lest you fall into a well.

He is a dog who sleeps idly before every door; and he is an ass who comes helplessly to every tent.

See from what side this love and envy enter the breast; do you know who informs the heart but a heart-cherisher?

Wait like a bird guardian over the egg, for from the breast's egg will be born drunkenness and union and laughter.

Only he has a skirt; all are beggars, uncle—clutch with both your hands his royal skirt.[169]

Like the sun go in grief for him into the fire till night; when it is night, gently turn about his roof like the moon.[170]

On his roof these stars are keeping watch till dawn; by Allāh, what a blessed presence, what an imperial court!

Those prophets who even in the earth turned their faces to heaven escaped from the snare of earth and the company of every fool;

They were snatched by that side like iron by a magnet, like a straw which flies without wings to amber.

Know that without His sending down no provision grows in the earth, without the society of His guiding form no substance can come into being.

The spirits are excited like camels by the cry, *"Travel!"*—like a Bedouin He cries, "Forward!" to those camels.

On the table of the heart the soothsayer casts the sand divination realities, so that through His figures the sand has become fine gold and pure.[171]

Go more gaily, fellow travelers, for a physician has come into the world who brings to life every dead one, gives sight to all who are blind.

All these things come to pass; but when his face lifts the veil, no Venus or melody remains, no "woe, woe" to the mourner.

Be silent, if you are a nightingale, go, fly back to the rosebush; the bolbol goes to the thornbed, but only rarely, from time to time.

313

Before this I sought a purchaser for my discourse, and now I wish of you to buy me from my words.

I have carved idols enough to beguile every person; now I am drunk with Abraham, I am sated with Āzar.[172]

An idol without color and scent arrived; my hand was put out of action by him. Seek another master for the shop of idol-making.

I have cleared the shop of myself, I have thrown away the idols; having realized the worth of madness, I have become free of thoughts.

If an image enters my heart I say, "Depart, you who lead astray!" If it displays grossness, I destroy its composition.

Who is suitable for Leylī? He who becomes Majnūn for her. That man is at the foot of the flag whose soul is on the other side.[173]

314

Do not fling stones at the factory of glassmaking, do not strike anew the wounded heart of the broken-hearted.

Strike all at my heart, for it is a pity and stupidity for your blows and strikes to strike another's breast and soul.

Free all the captives of cruelty save me, that on your servant you may look with cruelty.

I am happy whether you are faithful or cruel; may I never journey without you, either in fidelity or cruelty.

If your image has not entered the eye of a particular man, the eye of a slain ibex is dark and gazes wildly.

Before the world's prison I was with you wholly; would that I had never passed by this place of snares.

How often I have said, "I am happy. I will not go on a journey"; see this hard journey, the road from the heights to the earth.

Your grace deluded me, saying "Go, do not be afraid: my generosity shall be your escort, there shall be no danger to you.

"When you go into strange lands, you will have time to become mature; then you will return to your homeland with learning and accomplishment."

I said, "O soul of mine, what information shall I gain without you? Who goes from you for the sake of information? Only the uninformed.

"When I quaff wine from your hand, I am unaware and drunk and happy, without danger and fear of anyone, untroubled by any man."

He spoke words in my ear like the words of highwaymen; the king rolled me off my head, he bewitched me.

The story is long indeed—alas for the cunning and deceit, if this night his generosity does not show us any dawn.

315

You have come in order to expound my secret to all, to reveal and indicate that signless king.

Last night your drunken fantasy came cup in hand. I said, "I will not drink wine"; it said, "Do not, the more loss to you."

I said, "I fear if I drink, shame will fly from my head; I will reach out to your curls, and you will withdraw from me."

It saw that I was making airs and said, "Come, it is astonishing that when someone offers you his soul, you should frown on him.

"With all you are deceit and cheating; with the like of me would you be the cheat too? I am the provost of secrets; do you hide a secret from me?

"I am the treasure of the heart of earth; why do you lay your head on the earth? I am the qibla of heaven; why do you turn your face to heaven?[174]

"Look at the king who gives you the sight of vision; if you angrily turn your head away, you will do the same on the day of death.

"Be pale of cheek for him who gave you the color of your cheeks; why do you saffron your face for the sake of a shadow?

"Be like a cock, time-aware and leader; it would be a pity to make your cock into a hen.

"Sit crookedly but tell the truth; truth has its reward. I am your soul and spirit—do you depart to another?

"If like *Lend*, you lend [God] a clipping, you will turn half a clipping of counterfeit into a treasure and mine;[175]

"And if for two or three days you bandage your eyes with *Fear God*, you will make the fountain of your sensible eye into a sea of the pearl of vision.[176]

"If for a moment you go straight as an arrow at my target, you will make the shaft of the arrow of heaven a bow for your string.

"Is there any generosity better than this, that with your sins and guilt I should expound how you should lament before me?

"Enough for those words which will be written or not contained in the mouth; if you were to open every atom, you could make a mouth."

316

The sand has become satiated with the water; I have not become, bravo! No string in this world is there to fit my long bow.

The sea is my least draft, the mountain my least morsel; what a leviathan I am. O God! Open for me a way.

I am more thirsty than death, I writhe like hell; is not any good fat morsel coming to me, I wonder?

The lean one of love has no remedy but union; none is there but your hand to feed grass to the mouth of love.

Reason enters your trap and loses both head and beard, though it be heavy-headed or swift to leap.

You are the implanter of sincerity in the heart of every unitarian; you likewise print images in the heart of every anthropomorphist.

Noah from the zenith of your wave becomes mate of a raft; spirit from the scent of your street is drunk and dissolute and distraught.

Be silent, and return to the palace of the silent ones; you, cast in a village, return to the city of love.

317

Restless heart of mine, say, of what substance are you? Of fire? Of water? Of man? Of peri?

From what direction have you come? On what food pastured? What have you seen in nonexistence? Why are you flying thither?[177]

Why do you uproot me? Why aim at my destruction? Why cut the road of wisdom? Why tear your own veil?

All animals and living beings are weary of nothingness except you, who are carrying your baggage into nonentity.

You are going hot and hurrying, drunk, dissolute, to whose

counsel would you hearken? How long will you fall for the coquetry of men?

You are a torrent flowing, flowing from the mountaintop of this world towards the sea of no-place, faster than my breath.

Garden and spring are bewildered to know by what breeze you blow; lily and cypress are intoxicated with you: what a rose, what a narcissus you are!

The music of the tambourine whose hoop is not accompanied by tinkling cymbals, like the ravings of an unbeliever, enters not our ears.

The Moses of your love said to me "Become untouchable"; how do I not flee from all? How not run away from the Samaritan?[178]

I have fled from all, though I am in the midst of men, as the Ja'fari gold coin is in the midst of the earth of the mind.

Though the gold cries out two thousand times, "I am gold," till it leaves the mine, no one will purchase it.

318

Do not heap on yourself, lest you congeal; your snow will make you congeal even though you be the furnace of fire.

He who does not ferment of himself destroys your ferment; and he who kindles no fire, brotherhood does not come from him.

Look for his fatness with your hand, be not deceived by his wool; don't look at his head and moustaches, his soul is lean.

If this melody is joyful, leap up and advance ardently; do not make your head so-and-so, do not listen slackly and superficially.

319

I would have shown my face to you if I were not wholly soul; the sign of me would have been seen were I not without sign.

Silver of bosom, am I not gold? Ruby of lips, am I not jewel? I would have shown my gold-essence were I not in the mine.

Your grace does not let me, else I would drive away all the people of the world in desire of you, O sugar, like a fly.

The rosebush of the soul said to your love, "Did I not fear, I would be all tongue like the lily."

Men say, "You are a reasonable man, for a moment come to yourself." I reply, "If I were like this, for a moment I would be like that."

If the silver-robed moon were worthy of your street, I would take him by the waist and draw him along to you.

If the wave of passion for your love let me be for a moment, I would extinguish all fires and be the salvation of lovers.

If he had not sewed up my eye of time with the arrow of jealousy, I would be openly and visibly like a bow in his hand.

This is a symbol and metonymy for Tabriz and Shams-e Dīn; ah, how would it be if I had been an interpreter before him.

320

Passion for that Beloved brought me out of learning and reciting so that I became mad and distracted.

Once I took my way earnestly to prayer rug and mosque; I put on the shirt of abstinence to increase good works.

Love entered the mosque and said, "Right-guided master, rend the bond of being; why are you in bondage to prayer?

"Let not your heart tremble before the blow of my sword; lay down your neck, if you wish to journey from knowledge to vision.

"Do full justice to ruffianism, if you are a dissolute and drunkard; if you are lovely and beautiful, why do you remain behind the veil?

"Lovely ones may not flee from exhibiting their features; how can idols suffer not to indulge in coquetry and face decoration?

"Now through your face you have bestowed love and impatience on reason, now through your eyes played the Messiah to the sick;

"Now with your tresses given the image of God's cord to the believer, now through twisted curls given a cross to the Christian.

"If you have beheld your beauty which excels the sun, why have you withered and decayed in this dusty prison?

"Why do you not become refreshed by the graces of the heart's springtime? Why do you not laugh like the rose and pound ambergris?

"Why do you not ferment like wine in the vat of this world, that the fermenting may bring you forth from this enameled lid?

"Why is your Jacob denied the liberty of your lovely face? Joseph of the lovely ones, why do you languish in the bottom of the well?

"Behold your own beauty, ignorant one, in the light of the souls of the Pegs [*owtāds*], for the believer is the mirror of the believer in time of loneliness.[179]

"The earth sees its secrets in the face of the garden, 'What through its beauty and charm I have in my heart.'

"The rock sees its secret in the ruby and turquoise, 'I have a treasure in my heart yearning to emerge.'

"The dark iron sees its heart in the mirror, 'I am recipient to light, after all things bright.'

"When nonentities see how nonentities have been changed, they come into existence to enjoy a meeting.

"Would the fly have gone around to every dunghill had it known that by effort and virtue the 'Anqā comes out of its composition?[180]

"When the Sufi has become 'son of the moment,' he does not become an idle person tomorrow; that person soon becomes idle who is a fool and a procrastinator.[181]

"Sit among sweethearts if you are not immature and impotent; use yourself to lovers, my friend, do not wander about everywhere.

"Fish, it has become certain to you from the sea behind your back; turn your face round and go back, since you are a sea creature.

"Hear the call of *Return*, go to the water of life; enter the water and go gaily, why do you linger in water and clay?[182]

"With heart and soul you have gone to a place where neither soul nor heart remain; on your own foot you have gone to a place where you bite your own hand.[183]

"Become gold through the sun of eternity; go not to another's gold, for love of gold makes you yellow, though your face is silvery.

"The world says to you, 'Why have you become my slave? After all you are born of the king, it is I who should be your slave.'

"The sea says to you, 'I shall be your steed, rather than that you should be my steed, acting as porter and water-carrier.'[184]

"Be silent, I was like you too, but I kept silence and found rest; if you listen to me, you will be silent too, and find rest."

321

Today the king in secret visited the madmen; a shout went up from the souls of the spiritual distracted ones.

Amid the cries that king recognized my voice, for my voice had become purified of animal breaths.

He signaled so royally that the madmen leaped from his bonds; if I am mad, O king, you are the Solomon of the *dīvs*.[185]

O king, you share the secrets of the birds and the spells of the *dīvs;* now if it is fitting you should recite a spell on this madman.

An elder approached the king saying, "Bind him in chains, for this madman is causing enough disturbance and disorder in the *dīvān.*"

My king said, "This madman will accept no chain other than the chain of my tress; you do not know his character.

"He bursts thousands of bonds to fly to my hand; *to us returning* he becomes, for he is a royal falcon."[186]

322

There entered the city of man a mighty torrent; the heavens were destroyed, and a waterwheel of pure light was set turning.

That city was simply madness, mankind therein distracted; for he had escaped from yesterday and tomorrow, when he awakened from a sleep.

The water boiled and became a wind which caused every mountain to fly like straw before a fierce wind, hot and burning.

Having cleaved through the mountains, he revealed the mines, you could see ruby on ruby shining like moonlight.

In that glow you behold him, a Chinese moonface, his two hands of separation full of blood like the hands of a butcher.

From the scent of the blood of his hands all the spirits are drunk with him; all the skies abject before him—bravo, the gracious Giver!

When he slays, it is like the trampling of grapes that through perishing may become immortal, the grapes become syrup.

Though you trample hundreds of thousands of grapes, all will be one when such a door has been opened from the soul towards unification.

It is necessary that Shams-e Tabrīzī should take the hand of that soul, put the ring on his finger, bestow kingly apparatus.

323

Fire-worshiping heart of mine who spins like a ball in the fire, say to the *Sāqī*, "Quick now, a glass of lees to begin with!"[187]

Come, lip-biting *Sāqī*, cook with wine and raw ones; bravo, garden and orchard of vine from which you pressed the grapes!

I will give a hint which no one gives; the hint is this, O fair of stature, that on that night you transported me unselfed, you committed me over to that moonface of mine.

You, reason, do you remember how, when the king of reason out of love bestowed that fiery wine on me, at the first breath you died?

That darling brought two dishes, one of fire, one full of gold; if you take gold, it becomes fire, and if you set on fire, you win the game.

See the proud *Sāqī!* Extinguish that pretty fire! What do you know of the power of the fire, for there you are a little child?

Get out of the fire, you will rise happy out of Shams-al-dīn Tabrīzī; and if you flee into the gold, like gold you will have congealed.

324

My heart came like a pen in the fingers of the Beloved; tonight it is writing *zay*, tomorrow it will write *ray*.

He trims a pen for epistolary style, copying and the rest; the pen says, "I am resigned, you know; who am I, lord?

Now he blackens its face, now he rubs it in his hair; now he holds it upside down, now he uses it for a task.

On one sheet he cancels a world and makes it headless; on another sheet he delivers a [perilous] conjunction from calamity.

The splendor of the pen is according to the dignity of the scribe, whether it is in the hand of a king or a commander.

He splits its head for the reason he knows; Galen knows best what is best for the patient.

That pen is unable to utter by its own reason any applause; that pen knows not of its own nature to make disapproval.

Whether I call it pen or call it flag, in it is sense and senselessness—bravo, the conscious senseless one!

The mind can not compass its description, for in it is the union of opposites, a composition without composition, amazing!—constrained yet with free will.

325

By the right of old companionship and friendship, do not repeat to the Beloved all that I uttered last night, unconscious and sick;

But if, as God decrees, that moon hears of those things, he himself knows what a melancholy lover will say in the darkness of night.

When reason is not at home, the tale will be distorted—now low, now high, now war, now submissiveness.

If God should scatter my frenzy over the world, you will not see one man with reason; all will be stripped of their reason.

Reason, can it be that you pour these dark suggestions into me? Cloud, can it be you who rains upon me this troubled potion?

Muslims, Muslims, guard well your hearts; let none go about me, either to sightsee or to sympathize.

326

At dawn I said to that moon, "O I body and you soul, I am in this state that you see, and weep for what you know.

"You are beyond infidelity and faith, and drive a fast mount;

what a fearless king you are! Do precisely as you are.

"Just once return and pass our way, gaze on the thicket of the souls—behold the trees wet with blood, like branches of coral."

You have heard how a raw one gets a reputation among men, not fearing that self-will may stamp its brand on his forehead.

Do not disapprove of the pure ones; be afraid of the blow of the fearless ones—for the patience of the soul of the suffering ones will annihilate you utterly.

You who are selfed, do not wrestle with the unselfed; you enemy of the darvishes, do not mix in fight with them with a stratagem of which you are incapable;

For Shams-al-dīn Tabrīzī, with life-bestowing and blood-spilling, kindles the fire to a fierceness by Divine powers.

327

O spiritual form, why are you fleeing from us? You are after all of the house, you know the state of this servant.

By the right of my hot tears, by the right of my pale cheeks, by the bond that I have with you beyond this human phase—

Though the whole world were laughing, without you it were a prison; enough this, show compassion to this deprived prisoner.

Though I am with all my very dear ones, when you are afar I am sore distraught—O God, may such distraction not be the lot of anyone.

What shall I tie to that fleeing foot of yours so that you may not flee? You resemble an unfaithful soul; you are fleeing like our Beloved.

Though you gallop up out of the nine spheres and set fire to the seven seas, I will rend to pieces spheres and seas with love and patience and strength.

Even if like the sun you surmount the fourth heaven, I will still come secretly to your stirrup like a servant.

328

The physician of the soul brought a tray as a present; if you are a doting old man you will become fair and youthful.

It gives life to the body, intoxication to the soul; it takes away from the heart's slackness, from the cheeks' pallor.

That was the tray of Jesus, it became the inheritance of the physicians; you will find in it the antidote, if you have swallowed the poison of death.

You who seek that tray, turn your face to this qibla; when you turn your face thither, you will become the moonfaced of the world.

There is a pill hidden there which touches not the teeth, neither wet nor dry, neither hot nor cold.

Through that pill smaller than a grain you will come to the top of that dome, for that has become the dwelling place of Jesus; and that grain, for all its smallness,

Has become a protection, and every powerless man seeks the protection of your generosity; never will he whom you have nourished become lean.

I said to the physician of the soul, "Today in thousands of ways there is a sure footing, since you have trodden firmly."

He to whom you have given a place will never be by aught displaced; grief will not pare that heart which you have pared of grief.

Be silent and hush your words now that the test has befallen you; say farewell to pledges, you are free of those pledges.

329

My soul, why do you tarry so long in the land of exile? Return from this exile; how long will you be dispersed?

I sent a hundred letters, I signaled a hundred ways; either you do not know the way or you do not read the letter.

If you do not read the letter, the letter itself reads you; and if you do not know the way, you are in the grip of Him who knows the way.

Return, for in this prison no one knows your worth; sit not with the stonyhearted, for you are a gem of this mine.

You who have escaped from bond of soul, washed your hands of heart and soul, leaped from the snare of the world—return, for you are one of the falcons.

You are both water and stream and are seeking for water; you are both lion and deer and are better than they.

How far is it from you to the Soul? Are you more remarkable than the Soul? Are you commingled with the Soul, or a ray of the Beloved?

You are the light of the moon in the night, candy and sugar on the lip; dear lord, what a person you are! Dear lord, you are a divine marvel!

Every moment you bestow beauty and splendor, and we bestow heart and head and soul. Such a market is very fine—you give and take splendidly.

It is of your love to take away the life, of us to die like sugar; to eat poison from your hand is the very fountain of life.

330

Become of one hue with the community, that you may feel spiritual delight; enter the street of the tavern, that you may behold the dregs-drinkers.[188]

Drain the cup of passion, let it be that you become a disgrace; close up the eyes of your head, that you may see the secret eye.

Open your two hands if you desire an embrace; break the idol of clay, that you may see the face of the idols.[189]

How long for the sake of an old woman will you endure such a dowry? How long for the sake of three loaves will you face sword and spear?[190]

Lo, the *sāqī* who is no tyrant, in his assembly there is a circle— enter and sit in that circle; how long will you gaze on the circling of fate?

Here is a good bargain—give a life and receive a hundred; cease to act the wolf and dog, that you may behold the shepherd's love.

By night the Beloved goes about; do not take opium tonight, close your mouth against food, that you may feel the taste of the mouth.

You say, "The enemy took so-and-so away from me"; go, abandon so-and-so, that you may see twenty so-and-so's.

Think of naught but the creator of thought; thought for the Beloved is better than thinking about bread.

With the breadth of God's earth why have you clung to prison? Knot care less, that you may see the expanse of Paradise.[191]

Silence this speech, that you may gain speech one day; pass down from the soul and the world, that you may behold the Soul of the world.

331

You imprisoned in air nine spheres of emerald till you brought into orbit a form of earth.[192]

Water, what are you washing? Wind, what are you seeking? Thunder, why are you roaring? Spheres, why are you turning?

Love, why are you laughing? Reason, why are you binding? Patience, why are you content? Face, why are you pale?

What place is there for the head on the road of fidelity? What worth has life itself in the religion of manliness?

That man is perfect in quality who is the quarry of annihilation; there is room for not one hair in the circle of uniqueness.

Whether anguish or joy, it is far from freedom; cold is that person who remains in hotness and coldness.

Where is the gleam of the charming brow if you have seen my moon? Where is the gleam of drunkness if you have drunk spiritual wine?

Has not disquietude from this purse and that bowl seized you? After all you are not a blind ass; what are you circling around?

With the breast unwashed what profits it to wash the face? From greed you are like a broom, you are always in this dust.

Every day for me is Friday, and this sermon of mine is perpetual; this pulpit of mine is high, my screen is true manliness.

When the steps of this pulpit become empty of men, the spirits and the angels will bring a present from God.

332

Garden, do you know in whose wind you are dancing? You are pregnant with fruit, intoxicated with the rose bower.

Why do you possess this spirit, if you are this body? Why do you paint this image, if you are all soul?

What offering is life to you? Dates brought to Baṣra! How can I speak of you as a pearl, since you are the envy of Oman?[193]

Reason, wag your chin thiswise by your own analogy; what do you know of thatwise, being fascinated by [human] chins?

It is difficult to play the flute for the deaf, or to sprinkle sugar over the head of one suffering from the bile.

Faith borrows a hundred eyes to see him, until faith becomes drunk with that wine divine.

I fall at the foot of the heart; every day I say, "Your secret will be hidden unless you cause it to leap forth."

That six-sided dice is appropriate to that checkerboard; how shall the human dice be contained in any board?[194]

Shams-al-Ḥaqq Tabrīzī, why do I return every instant to your hand, if you are not the king?

333

How happy the day when you return from the road and shine in the window of the soul like the moon from above!

Behold that moon ever-waxing, devoid of all ornaments; you will adorn like the empyrean this earthly floor.

Many a fettered man of reason, who is escaped out of self; many a soul, which begins anew the rule of sugar-cracking,

Many a caravan without mount and provision will find, out of this six-cornered abode, the road into the placeless world.

Illuminate my soul, so that my soul says to my body, "Today regard me, you master of tomorrow!"

You are water, I am a stream; how should I seek to join you? The stream has no luster if you do not open the water.

You who are happy with being before—that is, being more than all; by Allāh, so long as you are with self, you will not find repose from self.

I was seeking the heart; on the road I saw it fallen into this melancholy passion, itself like a man suffering from the bile.

Shams-al-Ḥaqq Tabrīzī, your separation has filtered me; you will see nothing but love, though you filter me a hundred times.

334

If the knowledge of the tavern were your intimate companion, this [formal] knowledge and science would be mere wind and caprice in your eyes;[195]

And if the bird of the unseen cast its shadow upon you, the Sīmorḡ of the world would be but a fly in your sight.[196]

If the concourse-splendor of the king of reality displayed itself, this drum of the kings would be for you a jingling bell.

If the dawn of true felicity showed favor to you, how would your skirt and beard be in the hand of the night patrol?

If the leaders cast their protection on you, the thought that is before the heart would be behind.

If your heart's ear did not hear things contrariwise, one letter of the book of lovers would be enough.

He says, "All are dead, not one has returned"; if that fool saw one who had returned, he would be a somebody.

The flame of your soul is trembling at the cold wind of death; it would not be trembling if it had borrowed fire from immortality.

If your worthless nature were not a fellow traveler of the worthless, this fatal draft would be in your throat like a choking straw.

This child of your intelligence would have reached "Blessed is He"; in the school of happiness why are you stuck at "he frowned?"[197]

Silence, for all these things are dependent on the "moment"; if the "moment" were here, summons would come to your aid.

335

Become a lover, become a lover and bid jumping be gone; you are after all a king's son, how long will you be a prisoner?

To the king's son, the commandership and vizierate is all a disgrace; beware that you take nothing but love.

That one is not the commander of death, he is the prisoner of death; the whole passion for viziership is naught but a boredom.

If you are a picture on the bath, seek after the spirit; so long as you are in love with form, whence will you receive spirit?[198]

Do not mingle with dust, for you are a pure essence; do not mingle with vinegar, for you are sugar and milk.[199]

Though on this side people do not recognize you, on that side where side is not, how matchless and incomparable you are!

This world is death, and in this perishing world if you are not a prince, is it not enough that you do not die?

You are the lion of God in the form of man; that is evident in your attack and stateliness and courage.

Since I saw your learning and station and graces, I have become indifferent to the learning of the *Maqāmāt* of Ḥariri.

This life has become untimely; but since you exist in the light of God, what matters timely or late?

The measure of the beloved is the glory of the lover; helpless lover, behold of what grandeur are you and I.

The beauty of the moth is according to the measure of the candle; after all, are you not a moth of this light-living candle?

Shams-al-Ḥaqq Tabrīz, this is why you are invisible, because you are the very essence of sight, or the essence [eye] of the All-Seeing.

336

I found in my house a token of the king, a ring of ruby and a belt particular of the mine.

Last night I was asleep and he came, that heart-capturing king and spiritual confidant.

Last night my king broke two hundred cups and pots in rowdy, drunken fashion in the manner you know about.

You might say that out of drunkenness he chose my rook, for my rook is engaged on a secret business of the king.

Today the scent of the beautiful one is in this house, from this scent in every corner a beauty is visible.

The blood in my body is pure wine from that scent; every hair of me is a drunken pitch-black Hindu.

Give ear and listen to the drunken shout, these melodies of song from my lutelike stature.

Fire, wine and tent are as cash; the elders of the path receive their youth.

In the mirror of Shams-e Ḥaqq va Dīn, King of Tabriz; both the form and the whole is polished in the sea of realities.

337

I grant that you do not see the face of that Chinese girl; do you not see the moving of this veil proceeds from her moving?

Through the luster of that moon which is hidden in the skies, you have seen a hundred moons in earthly particles.

O leaf, scattered in the contrary wind, if you do not see the wind, do you not see that you are so?

If the wind is not stirred by thought, you do not stir; and if that wind does not sit still, you do not sit still.

The empyrean, heaven and spirit in this revolution of states are camels in file, and you are the hindermost.

Move upon yourself and drink of this blood, for in the womb of heaven you are a fetus-child.

In the sphere of your heart suddenly a pain arises; if you raise your head from the sphere, you know that you are not this.

Your ninth month is the face of Shams-al-Ḥaqq Tabrīz, O you who are the trustee of the trust of both worlds.

O heart, be patient in this blood until the ninth month; you are that month [moon], O king, for you are Shams-al-Ḥaqq va Dīn.

338

Heart, since you have become understanding of the mysteries, you have become useless for all other employments.

Be still mad and insane; why have you come to your senses and recovered your wits?

Meditation is all for the sake of acquiring; you have become entirely giving.

Preserve that same order of Majnūn, for you have become indifferent to all orderings.

If you desired to be veiled and prudent, why did you go about drunk in the market?

To sit in a corner yields you no profit once you have become the friend of the dissolutes of this path.

Go forth into the desert, that same desert where you were; you have wandered long enough in these ruins.

There is a tavern in your neighborhood, from the scent of its wine you have become intoxicated;

Seize this scent and go to the tavern, for you have become nimble-paced as that scent.

Go to the mountain of Qāf like the Sīmorḡ; why have you become the friend of owl and heron?[200]

Go like a lion into the thicket of reality; why have you become the friend of fox and hyena?

Go not after the scent of the shirt of Joseph, for like Jacob you are in mourning.

339

No interpreter of our fires, no Targum for the secrets of our hearts—

Heart and love have become naked of one hundred veils, soul and soul seated two and two—

If Gabriel himself would enter between the two, he would not have one moment's security from the fire.[201]

Every instant union upon union, on every side vision upon vision;

On whose roof you, seated as a watchman, see the kings of reality!

At the end of the thread of union with God is the Mount of Sinai which cannot endure this light for a single moment.

If you were to knot together a hundred universal reasons, there would be no ladder for this tall roof;

If I utter a sign of that signless one, the signs of all true men would be prostrated.

This word has become for you a present from that light which transcends the reach of words.

Words have become a belt for Shams-e Tabrīz; come, fasten it on, if you have a waist.

340

You have flown from this narrow cage, you have escaped from this prison of cutpurses.

You have removed dust from the mirror, you have seen on the mirror what you have seen.

You have heard reports of low and high; seen on high what you have heard.

Since you have committed water and clay to water and clay, you have carried the fabric of spirit to heaven.

You have leaped out of the revolutions of the body, you have reached the spiritual revolutions.

You have come out from the mother's womb that is this world, you have run to the intelligent father.

Every moment drink wine sweeter than life in exchange for every bitterness you have quaffed for our sake.

Choose and seize whatever you desire, since you have chosen us above all the world.

You have gone forth from the cooking pot of this world like sweetmeat, because you are now cooked for the table of that world.

Though the egg has become empty of your bird, you have flown beyond the egg of the world.

Hereafter you are not contained in this world, fly on yonder, for every moment you are augmenting.

Silence! Depart, for your lock has been opened; death has directed the key to your lock.

341

May these nuptials be blessed for us, may this marriage be blessed for us;[202]

May it be ever like milk and sugar, this marriage like wine and halvah.

May this marriage be blessed with leaves and fruits like the date tree;

May this marriage be laughing forever, today, tomorrow, like the houris of paradise.

May this marriage be the sign of compassion and the approval of happiness here and hereafter;

May this marriage be fair of fame, fair of face and fair of omen as the moon in the azure sky.

I have fallen silent, for words cannot describe how the spirit has mingled with this marriage.

342

Ho, water of life, turn me about like a mill with plenty.

So continue, that forever and ever my scattered heart may be in one place, I in another.

Twig and leaf move not save by a wind; straw-blade flies not without amber.

Since a straw moves not save by a wind, how shall the world move without desire?

All the parts of the world are lovers, and every part of the universe is drunk with encounter;[203]

Only they do not tell you their secrets—it is not proper to tell the secret save to one worthy.

The grazers, whose pasture grazes on the cup and table of the sweet lord.

Did not the ants tell their secret to Solomon, did not the mountain echo back to David?

Were this heaven not a lover, his breast would not be serene;

And if the sun had not been a lover, there would be no radiance in his beauty.

If earth and mountain were not lovers, no blade of grass would spring from their breasts;

If the sea were not aware of love, it would finally come to rest somewhere.

Be a lover, that you may know the lover; be faithful, that you may see the Faithful.

Heaven did not accept the burden of trust, for it was in love and afraid to make a mistake.[204]

343

I heard that you praised your servant—who am I? You have shown yourself such kindness.

You are the ruby-mine, the soul of amber; in compassion you assisted a blade of straw.

I was a worthless and valueless piece of iron; you polished me, made me a mirror.

You ransomed me from the flood of extinction, for you are both Noah and the Ark of Judi.

Heart, if you have burned, give scent like aloewood; if you are raw, then burn now, for you are firewood.

I slept under the shadow of fortune; you opened a way for me beside the five senses.

On that road it is possible to go to east and west, without feather, without head or foot.

On that road is no thorn of free will; no Christian is there, no Jew.

The soul, beyond the circumference of its blue sky, is escaped from blueness and blindness.

Why do you weep? Go to the laughing ones. Why do you tarry? Go to the same place where you once were.

From this honey, which has a hundred kinds of strings, see if you have received anything except boils?

344

In body you are with us, in heart you are in the meadow; you are the quarry yourself when attached to the hunt.

You are girdled here in the body like a reed, inwardly you are like a restless wind.

Your body is like the diver's clothes on the shore; you like a fish, your course is in the water.

In this sea are many bright veins, many veins too that are dark and black;

The brightness of the heart drives from those bright veins; you will discern them when you lift your wings.

In those veins you are hidden like the blood, and if I lay a finger, you are shy.

From those veins the voice of the sweet-veined lute is melancholy, reflecting the face of that melancholy.

Those melodies come from the shoreless sea which thunders like waves out of the infinite.

345

The springtide brings me into laughter, a hangover keeps me headspinning.[205]

A moon has brought me into the circle, a friend has made me friendless.

I have become as a string through the voice of a lute—the melody is audible, the string is invisible.

Like dust he stirred up the world; he has vanished like a wind in a dust.

That king lit up life like a spark who vanished in a spark as if burning.

That one adorned the beauty of the rose garden who vanished like a rose in the soul of a thorn.

My heart says, "Tell the *sāqī* my soul is drunk at least for that remaining one."

My heart like a mirror is silent and speaking in the hand of an amazing mirror-holder;

For when moment by moment there shines in the mirror an amazing figure of beauty.

Every form is as the Sultan's falcon; itself a quarry, it seeks a quarry.[206]

346

Do you not seek a sign of the separated ones? Where has gone that fidelity and affection?

The fishes are on this dry land of exile: come, water of the sea of life!

How long shall the fish remain out of its water? What am I to say? I do not know; you know.

Who am I to remain or not to remain? I desire you to remain in the world.

Let thousands of souls like me and better than me be your sacrifice, for you are the soul of the soul of the soul.

You say to me, "Be silent—have you not repented that you are leaving the road of tonguelessness?"

By the dust of your feet, I was not with myself out of drunkenness and wine and dizziness.

I am no better in silence than a vat; the wine does not remain hidden in the vat.

The wine of love is a more bubbling wine, for ordinary wine bubbles for a moment and this is ever-bubbling.

His face, red as the Judas blossom, does that which only a hundred jars of Judas-red wine can do.

I could describe his lips further but your mouth would burn if you were to recite it.

A stranger waterfowl is the lover's soul, bringing water as a present from fire;

Through fire, athirst, he discovered the joy of his water; fire makes a ladder to his water.

347

Where are you, martyrs divine, affliction-seekers of the plain of Karbala?[207]

Where are you, light-spirited lovers, speedier on wing than the birds of the air?

Where are you, celestial kings who know how to open heaven's gate?

Where are you, escaped from life and place? How can anyone tell reason, "Where are you?"

Where are you, you who have broken the door of the prison and set the debtors free?

Where are you, you who have opened the door of the storehouse? Where are you, help of the helpless?

You are in that sea whereof the world is the foam; swim a while more.

The forms of this world are the foam of that sea; leave the foam, if you are of the people of purity.

My heart foamed, which took the shape of words; let go the form and go take the heart, if you are of us.

Shams-e Tabrīzī, rise out of the east, for you are the source of the source of the source of every radiance.

348

Out of drunkenness and dissolution I have become such that I do not know earth from water.

I do not find anyone in this house—you are sober; come, perhaps you will find.

I only knew that the assembly set up first by you; I do not know if you are wine or kabob.

Inwardly you are the soul of the soul of the soul, outwardly you are the sun of the sun.

You are sweet-enchanting for you are the Messiah; you burn up *dīvs* for you are a meteor.

Make me happy-tempered for you make the garden laugh, though to the thirsty you are torture.

Come, see the numerous drunkards in the *bazar*, if you are a bailiff and making a census.

Like beggars for bread now questioning, like sufferers now responding.

Your smile is brief as a lightning flash, so you are a prisoner in the shadows of the clouds.

Enter the assembly of the Eternal being; behold circulating the *porringers like water troughs.*[208]

You are a lovely ruby, but you are in the mine; you are very beautiful, but you are in the veil.

If to the king you fly, you are the white falcon; if to the graveyard you fly, you are the raven.

Youthful of furtune, clap hands and say, "Youth, O youth, O youth!"

Say no word to anyone, if he presses you hard; only say, "God knows best what is right."

349

The garden is here, springtime, and the tall cypress—we will not go back from these surroundings.

Open the veil and close the door; here are we, you and I, and the empty house.

Today I am the special companion of love, having seized the cup of I-do-not-care.

Minstrel sweet of melody, sweet of reed, you must lament mighty sweetly.

Sāqī, joyous and happy, bring the wine forward immediately

That we may drink happily and sleep sweetly in the shadow of eternal grace—

Drink not by way of throat and stomach, sleep not as the result of nights.

O heart, I desire you to rub that cup upon your eyes;

When you become completely annihilated in the wine, that hour you are perfect existence.

You will remain constant from *He gave them to drink,* without death and annihilation and transfer.[209]

Give up thievishness, and go around happily, secure from the governor's tortures.

You say, "Show where security is"; go, go, for still you are questioning!

O day of such happiness, what day are you? O day, you are better than a thousand years.

All days are your slaves; they are separation, you are union.

O day, who shall behold your beauty? O day, you are tremendous in beauty.

You behold your own beauty, and that eye whose ear you box!

O day, you are not day from the sun; you are day through the light of the All-Glorious.

Every evening the sun prostrates itself; it begs for quittance of your moon.

O day, hidden in the middle of the day, O day, you abide eternally.

O daily bread of days and nights, O gentleness of north and south winds,

I will be silent from speaking of perfection, for you are beyond every perfection.

You become not manifest in words, for you are more manifest than all discourse;

By words spoken thoughts become manifest—you are above imagination and thought,

And that imagination and thought are athirst for you, you who have given smoothness to water.

Both of these are dry-mouthed in the water of spirit; in the world full, of self empty.

The rest of the ode is veiled from you behind the curtain, for you are aweary.

350

When you are aiming at brotherhood, first of all you must wash your face;

If your head is splitting with drunkenness, do not seek to split the heads of your brothers.

Either drive away the smell of your armpits, or say farewell to the beloved's embrace.

In the feast of a moon with hyacinth tresses how should it be etiquette for you to lament?

You want a quarry without a snare; be sure that like me you are seeking the impossible.

If your ears are hot from drunkenness, you are a Sufi of the concert of riotous ecstasy.

If your mind is unconscious of your ears, you are not single, you are a thousandfold.

351

The assembly is like a lamp, and you are like water; the lamp is ruined by water.

The sun has shone upon the gathering; depart from the midst, for you are as a cloud.

Sit not at the table, for you are raw; where is the smell of kabob, if you are kabob?

You went ahead, saying, "I am the chamberlain"; by Allāh, you are not the chamberlain, you are the curtain.

Since chamberlains of doors have indications, they know to what door they belong.

You are mounted on a wooden horse and stupidly rush to danger.

Either choose love, which is triple cash-in-hand, or choose abstinence, if you seek after the reward.

Sit and rise with the wakeful ones, for this caravan has departed and you are asleep.

Through Sams-al-dīn you will arrive at the stage, and in Tabriz you will find the way.

352

Union with you is the source of happiness, for those are but forms and this is reality.

Break not for a moment from your servant, for a ship cannot sail without water.

I am a faulty Qur'an but am made correct when you recite.

A Joseph alone, and a hundred wolves, yet he escapes when you are shepherd.

Every time you ask me, "How are you?" I am with tears and pale cheeks.

For the vulgar these two are tokens; what are signs to you who are without sign?

Unspoken you hear the discourse, unwritten you read the deed.

Without sleep you show visions, without water you drive on the ships.

Silence, have done with praises and petitions, for from the unseen has come *thou shall not see me.*[210]

353

I said to my heart, "Why are you thus? How long will you consort with love?"

The heart said, "Why do you not also come to experience the delights of love?"

Even if you are the water of life, how shall you choose aught but the fire of love?

You in subtlety have become as the wind, you are full of wine as the bumper glass.[211]

Like water, you give life to images; like a mirror, you are a trustee of beauty.

Every mean soul that has not those properties may think that you are the same—

O you who are the soul of heaven, even though in form you are of earth.

O fine-crumbled as *sorma,* you are the *sorma* of the eye of certainty.[212]

O ruby, of which mine are you? Enter the ring, for you are a fine signet.

A thousand compassions are ashamed before you the moment you are full of wrath as a sword.

Shams-e Tabrīz, your form is lovely, and what a sweet source you are in meaning!

354

Bird of heart, fly not save in the air of selflessness; candle of soul, shine not save in the palace of selflessness.

May the sun of God's grace ever shine upon lovers, so that the shadow of the phoenix of selflessness may fall upon all.

Though a lover may behold myriad fortunes and comforts, naught enters his vision save the calamity of selflessness.

Look upon me, who have cast myself into affliction for the sweetnesses I have experienced in the nonentity of selflessness.

What a life, what a hundred lives indeed, if a man should sacrifice them in desire for selflessness and for the sake of selflessness.

Lover, sit not with sorrowful ones, lest dust should fall on the joy of selflessness.

Use cruelly anyone who is a lover of prudence that you may find new pleasures in the faithfulness of selflessness.

When you know selflessness, leadership loses its market for you; head and leadership are as the dust of the foot of selflessness.

It is pleasant to get visibly on the throne of kingship over our enemies, but true things have no worth in comparison with selflessness.

If you wish that Shams-e Tabrīz should be your guest, empty your house of self, O landlord of selflessness.

355

You who let a garden go for the sake of a small fig, let slip the houri for the sake of an unworthy crone.

I am rending my shirt, and repulsion comes over me from the glance that a crone cast at a youth.

A stinking-mouthed crone with a hundred clutching talons and tricks, putting her head down from the roof to snare a clever one.

Who is such a crone? A savorless deception, fold on fold like an onion, fetid as garlic.

A prince has become her captive, pledged his belt—she laughs in secret, "Fool of a princeling!"

No full blossom is the garden of her beauty, no milk in the breasts of fidelity of that whore.

When death opens your eyes, then you will behold her, her face like the back of a lizard, her body black as pitch.

Now be silent, give no more counsel. The master's bond is very strong; the chain of his love draws without the help of a miserable chain.

356

Proclaim, O crier, at the head of every market, "Have you seen, Muslims, a runaway slave?

"A slave moonfaced, musk-scented, a troublemaker—swift of pace in time of coquetry, in time of peace slow.

"A boy, ruby-robed, charming of countenance, sugar-sweet, cypress-stature, saucy-eyed, acute, perfectly poised;

"In his bosom a rebec, in his hand a plucker; he plays a sweet air, charming, well-seated.

"Does anyone have a fruit of the garden of his beauty? Or a bunch of roses to smell from the rose bed of his loveliness?

"A Joseph by whose price the king of Egypt was bankrupted, on every side heart-wounded ones like Jacob by his glance.

"I will give freely my sweet life as lawful to whomever brings me a sign of him, or even a veiled hint."

357

"Ah, from those lightning-casting, sweet, mischievous cheeks! A thunderbolt from its lightning has fallen on the soul of every helpless one!"

When before the row of pearls and rubies shone like fire, a sea of pearls surged out of the rock.

This heart torn into a hundred pieces gave a piece to the door-keeper of the soul; when he emerged in the heart of the curtain, it became a better piece.

Paradise is divided into eight heavens, and one like a scroll;

behold the eight scrolls contained in a sheet of a cheek.

What kind of bird is this heart of mine, kneeling like a camel, or fire-eating like an ostrich around a blaze![213]

Quarry of joy, this heart of mine shared the same shop with your love; it found a fine colleague and fellow-worker in that shop.

Through the sun of your love, the motes of the souls have become like the moon, and every moment a star of felicity comes into the sky.

Your form is invisible, yet relates every detail—like the Messiah through the light of Mary, the spirit of God in the cradle.

Shams-e Tabrīzī, what inconsistency is there in the heart's states, at once abiding in love and fugitive from love?

358

Soul of a hundred rose gardens, you have vanished from jasmine; soul of the soul of my soul, why have you vanished from me?

Since heaven through you is resplendent, what is veiled to you? Since the body through you is living, how have you vanished from the body?

Out of the perfection of God's jealousy and the loveliness of your beauty, O king of men, you have thus vanished from men and women.

Candle of the nine skies, for you have passed through the nine skies, what secret is this, that you have vanished in the candle-holder?

O Canopus, before whose face the sun fainted, it is good, it is good that you have vanished from Yemen.[214]

Musk of Tartary makes a sign to mankind with every breath because you are the king of Cathay and have vanished from Kotan.[215]

What wonder, if you vanish from us and the two worlds, O selfless moon that has vanished from self?

O manifestation of souls, you have vanished in suchwise that out of exceeding hiddenness you have vanished from vanishing.

Shams-e Tabrīzī, like Joseph you have gone into the well; water of life, how have you vanished from the rope?

359

What a joyous pleasure it will be, what a charming spectacle, when such a part returns to the source of the source!

Wine will come from every side to its hand, without a cup, from every side to its eye, a darling, enchanting fair—

A darling who, did the granite rock catch secret of her ruby, the granite rock would receive life and become conscious.

The wine stole one attribute from the lips of my darling; inevitably the soul became a wine-bibber for the love of those lips.

In dawn a monk went along with me on the way to the monastery; I saw him a fellow-sufferer and fellow-worker with myself.

He brought to me, that auspicious companion, a bowl—from that bowl my soul became out of itself, a drunkard.

In the middle of my unselfedness the Tabriz of Shams-al-dīn displayed succor for the helpless ones in unity with Him.

360

Happy the moment when with compassion you scratch the head of lovers, happy the moment when from autumn arises the wind of spring.

Happy the moment when you say, "Come, poor lover, for you are distracted by me, you have no regard for others."

Happy the moment when he clings to the skirt of your grace and you say, "What do you want of me, wasted drunkard?"

Happy the moment when that *sāqī* of the assembly issues an invitation, when the cup of wine rides on the hand of the *sāqī*.

The particles of our bodies will be happy through that immortal wine; this greedy body will escape from the grief of eating at tables.

Happy the moment when the Beloved demands contributions from the drunkards, takes pledge from us with sweet and lovely cheeks.

Happy the moment when in drunkenness the tip of your tress is confused, the helpless heart passionately takes to curl-counting.

Happy the moment when the heart says to you, "I have no

plantation," and you say, "Whatever you plant shall grow for you."

Happy the moment when the night of separation says, "Good-night"; happy the moment when that springtide light shall give greeting.

Happy the moment when the cloud of divine grace comes in the air, from that cloud you rain pearls of grace on the desert.

This earth, which is thirstier than that black sand, shall swallow the water of life completely and make no dust.

Love has entered upon us with cups and wine; drunkenness has appeared to us from a hidden beloved.

A discourse surged like waves scattering pearls, it is necessary to silence it, since you do not let it pass into here.

361

When I reached your city you withdrew into a corner from me; when I left your city you did not give me a good-bye glance.

Whether you choose kindness or incline to rancor, you are all the soul's ease, you are all the feast's decoration.

The cause of your jealousy is that you are hidden, otherwise you are evident as the sun, for you are manifest through every mote.[216]

If you choose to be in a corner, you are darling of the heart and a prince; and if you rend the veil, you have rent the veils of all.

The heart of unbelief by you is confounded, the heart of faith by your wine is happy; you have robbed all of their sense, you have pulled the ears of all.

All roses are a prey to December, all heads in pawn to wine; you have redeemed both these and those from the hand of death.

Since there is no constancy in the rose, since there is no way to the rose, on you only is trust to be put; you are the stay and support.

If a few have cut their heads on account of Joseph's face, you have deprived two hundred Josephs of the spirit of heart and reason.[217]

You fashion the form of a person from filth and blood, that he may flee two parsangs from the odor of foulness.

You make him a morsel of dust to become pure herbage—he escapes from foulness when you have breathed spirit into him.

Come, heart, go to heaven, go to God's pasture, since you have grazed awhile in the pasture of cattle.

Set all your desire on that of which you have no hope, for out of original hopelessness you have reached thus far.[218]

Be silent, that the lord who bestows words may speak; for He made the door and the lock, and He also made a key.

362

Tidings are newly arrived—do you perhaps have no news of it? The envious heart has turned to blood; perhaps you have no heart.

The moon has shown his face, opened the wings of light; borrow a heart and eyes from someone if you do not have any.

Amazing, night and day a flying arrow comes from the hidden bow; yield your life to this arrow. What can you do? You have no shield.

Has not the copper of your being been changed, like Moses, to gold by His alchemy? What care? Though you have no gold in your bag like Korah?[219]

Within you is an Egypt whose sugarcane bed you are; what care, though you have no supply of sugar from without?[220]

You have become the slave of form, like the idol-worshipers; you are like Joseph, but within you do not gaze.

By God, when you see your own beauty in the mirror you will be your own idol, you will not pass over to anyone.[221]

O Reason, are you not unjust to call him like the moon? Why do you call him moon? Perhaps you have no sight.

Your head is like a lamp containing six wicks; from what are all six alight, if you have not that spark?[222]

Your body is like a camel which travels to the Kaaba of the heart; out of assishness you have not gone on the pilgrimage, not because you have no ass.[223]

If you have not gone to the Kaaba, felicity will draw you on; do not flee, idler, for you have no means of passing from God.

363

Ho, watchman of the dwelling, what sort of watchman are you? For the night-thief secretly carries off all our baggage.

Throw cold water on your face, rise up and make a tumult, for because of your sleepiness all our profit has been turned to loss.

Night and the sleep of watchmen are a thief's lamp; why do you not extinguish their lamp with a breath?

Give over being idle; be a night-traveler like the stars. What do you fear of earthly beings, since you are a celestial rider?

Two or three barks of a dog do not cut off the road to horsemen; what shall a dog or a hay-fed ox snatch from a fierce lion?

What effect have the dog of wrath and the ox of lust on a lion who rends asunder the ranks of vision in the thicket of realities?

Were you not two drops of water, that now you make an ark and a Noah to run to left and right midst the waves of the flood?[224]

Since God is your protection, what peril threatens the road for you? Your cap reaches the sky, for you are the head of all heads.[225]

What an excellent path it is, with God as companion; the hard journey would become like eternal Paradise.

Do not say, "What present shall I bring as a token?" Their own face is enough as a present to the sun and moon.

Whether you go or not, your felicity is running, discharging all the business in tranquillity and love.

When fortune is your slave it does you a thousand services, for it cannot do without you, even though you drive it from the door.

Sleep sweetly, for luck does not sleep on your account; take a stone in your hand, for it will become a ruby of the mine.

Mount heaven like Jesus; say, *let me see* like Moses, for God will not say to you, "Silence, thou shall not see Me."[226]

Silence, O heart; yet what use, if you block the lid of the jar? The heart of the vat will split when those truths ferment.

Every moment two thousand times you will recite this poem, if you realize how it travels beyond realities.

364

O idol, you are so subtle that you enter into our soul; O idol, by the right of your face, pray enter amongst us.

You possess the true world, you have not your home on earth; what would it be if for a time you entered our world?

You are subtle and without mark, you are hidden even from the hidden; this hiddenness of mine shines forth when you enter our hidden part.

Since you possess the speech of all birds, Solomon, what honey you impart to the lip when you enter our tongue!

In the world you alone are king, no one draws your bow; I will fly like an arrow if you enter our bow.

Parade forth, Shams-e Tabrīz, for you are the touchstone of God; all our copper turns to gold when you enter our mine.

365

You have the attribute of God; when you enter any breast, you display from that breast the glow of Mount Sinai.

You have the attribute of a lamp; when you enter a house by night, all the house receives light from the splendor of your brightness.

You have the attribute of wine; when you are in an assembly you kindle two thousand tumults and riots with your sweet graciousness.

When joy is fled, when passion is flown, what grasses and roses grow when you sweetly act the water-carrier!

When the world is frozen, when gaiety is dead, what other worlds you open out of the unseen!

From you comes this importunity in the heart of the restless ones; otherwise what acquaintance would dark earth have with brightness?

You are the sky about the earth revolving night and day; O sky, what do you want of us? Are you not the source of all light?

Now you scatter rain, now you sift the earth; you are not a seeker of filings, after all, you are all mine and touchstone.

Like men seeking filings night and day you sift the earth; why do you worship earth? Are you not the qibla of all prayers?

What wonder if a beggar seeks a gift from a king? This is the wonder—that a king begs from a beggar.

Even more amazing is this—the king has gone so far in petition that the beggar falls into error and thinks he is king.

Sky, are you not king? Is not the earth your slave? Then why are you in the air night and day serving the earth?

The sky answers me, "No one moves without reason; if a straw flies, that is due to some amber."

My words are meat to the angels; if I speak no words, the hungry angels say, "Speak, why are you silent?"

You are not of the angels, what do you know of angels' food? What should you make of manna? You deserve chives.

What do you know of this pottage that comes from the kitchen of the brain, when God acts the householder night and day?
Tabriz, say to Shams-al-dīn, "Turn your face to us." I err—say, "O sun, all face without a back!"[227]

366

My idol scolds, saying, "Why have you fallen in the middle of the road?" Idol, why should I not fall from such a wine as you have given me?

Idol, I fell in suchwise that even at the resurrection I shall not rise, when you held such a cup and uncovered such a flask.

I am dissolute, yet I have a little understanding, for you took up my head and placed it in your bosom.

Idol, from your drunken eye which is the wine-holder of love, you give wine without a cup—what a mighty master you are!

It is of your generosity, too, that the wine has swept away my reason, for if it still kept its reason, it should burst with happiness.

You gave me a bowl so that I am clapping my hands, for with one cup I escaped from one thousand undesirable things.

By your two ravishing drunken eyes for which joy was born, you are the primal spirit, for you were not born of any man.[228]

367

Since it has become certain to my heart that you are the soul of the soul of the soul, open the door of grace, for you are the stay of a thousand worlds.

When separation has become rebellious, you sweetly smite its neck in retribution for your loves, for you are the sword of the age.

When union has become lean, nourish it with the goblet; everything before you attains nourishment gratis.

Your sun has at last entered Aries in felicity, for the ancient world discovers from you the glow of youth.

What concerts are in the soul, what flagons pouring, which are reaching the ear from that tambourine and harp and songs!

How full is this rose bower with the song of the nightingale, so that from the riotous shouts of the drunkards you cannot tell wine from bowl.

All the branches are in flower, the kings have seized the cup; all have departed out of themselves through the heavenly wine.

Convey my soul's greetings to those kings, but you will not find anyone sober to convey my greetings to them.

The gnat has quaffed wine and lost its head and beard [feather], and annihilated Nimrod with a dagger.[229]

If the wine does this to a gnat, say, what will it do to an elephant? What shall I do? The wine of placeless land cannot be described.

From his life-gracing wine his dog of the cave is his lion-seizer which does nothing but act the shepherd around the cavern of the drunkards.[230]

If a dog has become so beside itself, consider what the raging lion, when it is faithful, discovers from the wine of those vessels.

Tabriz has become an East through the rising of Shams-al-dīn, for sparks reach the stars of spiritual truths from him.

368

Go, love, for you have become the most perfect of the lovely ones; you have smitten the necks of penitence and the penitent.

What can one rely upon with your love?—for you are such a thunderbolt. Who can associate with you?—for you are all brawling.

Neither earth nor heaven can stand or withstand you; you are not in their six directions, so whence have you come?

The eight paradises are in love with you; how beautiful is your face! The seven hells tremble at you; what a fire temple you are![231]

Hell says to you, "Pass, for I cannot endure you." You are the Paradise of Paradise and were the Hell of Hell.[232]

Lovers' eyes are wet on their skirts because of your sweet eyes; you are the provocation and brigand of every ascetic man and woman.

To be without you in the cloister is nothing but madness, for you are the very life of the cloister and temple.

Give justice to my ruined heart, O judge of love!—for you have taken tribute from my ruined village.

Simple heart of mine, from whom do you seek justice? It is lawful to love to shed blood, if you are of this guild.

Justice for lovers is beyond the bounds of the soul; you are engaged in useless thought and fancy.

Only the angels' attributes are privy to love for sure; you are a prisoner of the attributes of donkey and *dīv* and wild beast.

Enough, practice not magic; first deliver yourself, for you are the prisoner of the passion for magic and jugglery.

369

Gaze on the cheeks of love that you may gain the attributes of true men; sit not with the cold ones so you will not be chilled by their breath.

From the cheeks of love seek something other than the form; your business is to be a fellow sufferer with love.

If you have the attributes of a clod, you will never fly in the air; you will fly in the air if you break to pieces and become dust.

If you do not break to pieces, he who composed you will break you; when death breaks you, how will you become a unique pearl?

When a leaf becomes yellow, the fresh root makes it green; why are you content with a love from which you turn yellow?

370

Go, nimble-rising soul go on a strange journey to the sea of meanings, for you are a precious pearl.

If you remember, you have passed through water and clay; do not be vexed that you are passing from this terrace too.

Wash your wings of this water and clay, and become light and nimble; what are you doing not to fly in the wake of your friends who have flown?

Ho, break the pitcher and enter the river, O water of life; before every pitcher-breaker how long will you be the potter?

From this mountaintop go like a torrent towards the sea, for this mountain to no one's body offers an abiding-place.

Enough, cut not away from the Sun either to East or West, for through him you are now a crescent, now as a moon at the full.

371

By the right and sanctity of that, that you are the soul of all men, fill a cup with that whose description you know well.

Turn everything upside down, leave neither up nor down, so that men may know that today you are in this *meydān*.[233]

Strike the fire of wine in the chattel of shyness and shame; the drunkards' hearts are weary of secret joy.

The time has come for you to bring back to us that departed heart, that you should set our reasons aflying like your doves.

You are speaking subtleties in the ring of dissolute drunkards; it is fine when the treasure shines out in a ruin.

Circumambulate the fermented wine among these consumed ones; place before the raw ones that fricassee and eggplant concoction.

What has become of me? You tell me, for how should I know what has become of me, your lips utter [those] words so easily.

372

With such a gait, when will you reach the station? With such a habit, how will you gain the goal?

You are very heavy of soul and camel-hearted; when will you arrive among the nimble-spirited?[234]

With such grossness how will you be modest? With such a
joining [attachment for the world], how will you reach the one
who enjoys the union?

Since there is no broadness in the mind, how will you achieve
the society of the difficult secret?[235]

You are like water left in this clay; so how will you attain the
pure from water and clay?

Disregard the sun and moon like Abraham, else how will you
attain the perfect sun?[236]

Since you are weak, go, flee to the grace of God, for without
the Gracious how will you attain the excellence?

Without the tender care of that sea of loving kindness, how
will you reach the shore of such a wave?

Without the Borāq of love and the labor of Gabriel how will
you like Moḥammad attain all the stages?[237]

You take shelter in those who are without shelter; how will
you attain the shelter of the welcoming king?

Before *besmellāh* sacrifice yourself utterly; else, when you lie
dead, how will you attain the Name of God?[238]

373

Once more you have resolved to go, once more you have made
your heart like iron.

No, do not extinguish the lamp of our friendship; you have
poured oil into our lamp.

By Allāh, you have filled this world with rose and eglantine
and lily of your own face.

By Allāh, let no enemy say you are a friend who did the
enemy's work.

By Allāh, keep your servants together, you who have bright-
ened the world.

Once more you are laying on one side the love-plays you did
with me.

By Allāh, you have purified the skirt of the evil spirit by the
scatter of your sleeves.[239]

Mine of goldminters, Ṣalāḥ-al-dīn, like the moon you have
made a harvest of silver.[240]

374

O, you who have shaken a whole world, the voice of the reed, the voice of the reed, the voice of the reed.

What is the reed? To that beloved of the sweet kiss the place to kiss, the place to kiss, the place to kiss.

That reed without hand and foot fetches from men hand and foot, hand and foot, hand and foot.

The reed is a pretext; this is not the responsibility of the reed, this is nothing but the sound of the wing of that phoenix.

God Himself it is; what is all this veil? It is drawing the people of God to God.

We are beggars, *God is the All-Sufficient;* know, what you see of the beggar is due to the rich.[241]

We are all darkness except *God is light:* from the sun came the rays of this abode.[242]

Since the light in the house is mingled with shadow, if you desire the light, come out of the house to the roof.

Now you are happy, now depressed; if you do not want a depressed heart, depart out of this depression.

375

You are putting me on trial; O love, you know my weakness, yet you go on doing so.

You are becoming the interpreter of the enemy's secret; you implant mistaken thoughts in his heart.

You are setting fire to the thicket, and at the same time uttering complaints.

It may be thought that you have been cruelly wronged, you are making uproar and complaint like the weak.

You are the sun—who will oppress you? You do whatever you desire from on high.

You make us envious of one another; you make our quarreling into a fine spectacle.

To the gnostics you give wine as cash-in-hand; the ascetics you make drunk with tomorrow.

You give sorrow to the death-meditating bird; the bolbols you make drunk and singing.

You make the raven desirous of dung; your parrot you make sugar-cracking.

The one you draw into mine and mountain, the other you set face to the sea.

You lead us to happiness by way of suffering, or else you recompense our slip.

In this sea all is profit and justice; you dispense all beneficence and kindness.

This is the head of the subtlety; you speak its end, though you make us be without foot and head.[243]

376

Welcome, melody—you are that melody which has brought a sign from the spiritual world.

Pass by the ear and strike upon our souls, for you are the life of this dead world.

Ravish the soul and go aloft into that world where you have carried the heart.

Your laughing moon bears evidence that you have quaffed that heavenly wine.

Your sweet soul gives a sign that you were nourished in honey from *Alast*.[244]

Blades have begun to sprout from the earth to show the sowings that you have made.

377

You are both candle and fair one and wine, likewise spring in the midst of December.

Every side through love of you is one with feathers ablaze, the sun, and myriads like him.

Since your fire always falls upon the reed, sugar has gone through this passion into the soul of the reed.[245]

You have beheaded myriads with love so that the soul has not the strength to say, "Ah, alas!"

The lovers have built from the evil of the eye underground houses like the city of Ray.[246]

There is no worse torture than knowledge; alas for him who remains in good and evil.

Those women of Egypt in their unselfedness suffered wounds and did not utter "Woe!"

The king in unselfedness on the night of Ascension traversed a road of a hundred thousand years.

With the wind of selflessness break the prison of bone and sinew and tendon.

Shams-e Tabrīzī, annihilate us, for you are as the snow and we are as the shadow.

378

Do you know where you have come? From the midst of all-glorious sanctuary.

Do you not remember at all those happy spiritual stages?

Those things have become forgotten by you, so necessarily you are bewildered and distraught.

You sell my soul for a handful of dust; what kind of bargain and sale is this?

Give back the dust, and know your own worth; you are not a slave, you are a king, an emperor.

For your sake there came out of heaven the fair-faced ones, the sweetly hidden.

379

You who are imam of love, say *Allāh Akbar*, for you are drunk; shake your two hands, become indifferent to existence.[247]

You were fixed to a time, you made haste; the time of prayer has come. Leap up—why are you seated?

In hope of the qibla of God you carve a hundred qibla; in hope of that idol's love you worship a hundred idols.

Fly upwards, O soul, O obedient soul; the moon is above, the shadow is low.

Do not like a beggar knock your hand at any door; knock at the ring of the door of heaven, for you have a long hand.

Since the flagon of heaven has made you like that, be a stranger to the world, for you have escaped out of self.

I say to you, "How are you?" No one ever says to the "how-less" soul, "How are you?"

Tonight you are drunk and dissolute, come tomorrow and you will see what bags you have torn, what glasses you have broken.

Every glass I have broken was my trust in you, for myriadwise you have bound up the broken.

O secret artist, in the depths of your soul you have a thousand forms, apart from the moon and the Lady of the Moon [Mahastī].[248]

If you have stolen the ring, you have opened a thousand throats; if you have wounded a breast, you have given a hundred souls and hearts.

I have gone mad; whatever I say in madness, quickly say, "Yes, yes," if you are privy to *Alast*.

380

In the battle ranks we have no shield before our face; in the concert we are unaware of reed pipe and tambourine.

We are naught in his love, dust at the foot of his love; we are love fold upon fold, we are all love, nothing else.

When we have obliterated ourselves we become altogether love; when *sormah* is pounded, it is nothing but the source of sight.

Every body that has become an accident has become the soul and heat of self-interest; melt of all sicknesses, there is nothing worse than being congealed.

Out of desire of that melting and love for that cherishing the liver within me has turned all to blood; I have no liver any more.

My heart is broken into a hundred pieces, my heart has become astray; today if you search, there is no trace of heart in me.

Look at the orb of the moon, waning every day, so that in the dark period you might say there is no moon in the sky.

The changelessness of that moon derives from nearness to the sun; when afar, it is full-bodied, but such initiative does not belong to it.

O king, for the sake of the souls send Venus as a minstrel;

this soft pipe and tambourine are no match for the concert of the souls.

No, no—for what is Venus when the Sun itself is powerless? To be suitable for such ardor is not in the power of any lute or sun.

381

Yesterday you made compact and repentance, today you have broken them; yesterday you were a bitter sea, today you are a pearl.

Yesterday you were Bāyazīd and were augmenting; today you are in ruins, a dregs-seller and drunk.[249]

Drink the dregs, O soul! Break from reason, O soul! Do not wear blue, O soul, until you worship idols.[250]

Today you are very dissolute, you share the cup with the sun; You are not the master of the moon, nor the husband of the lady.[251]

You are greater than dwellings, you are outside mines; you are not that, but you are just as you are.

One corner you were bound up, of that corner you were sick; you opened that which was bound and escaped wholly, escaped.

A beast is not a rider, it is only for the sake of labor; you are no beast, you are a living man and you have leaped from labor, leaped.

You are a heavenly messenger; how can you be like the moon until you ride aloft and are in the hand of the thumbstall?

Silence, give no sign, though you expressed everything; every wounded one you have wounded has become the salve of a world.

382

Minstrel, when you draw your plectrums over the strings, you draw into labor these idlers of the way.

Love, when you enter, you draw these tarriers in the world of separation to the Beloved.

Despite the highwaymen you make the world secure, you drag to the gallows the thieves of the heart city.

You see the cunning schemer, and cunningly blind him; when you are the friend, you draw him into the cave.

You bind a golden saddle on the nimble-footed horses; the evil pack-horses you draw to the baggage.

You cherish our melancholic ones every moment; our market-minded ones you drag very miserably.

To the thorn-enduring lovers you show the rose bower; you draw into the thorns the self-willed whose joy is but for a moment.

To him who enters the fire you give access to the water; he who runs to water, you drag him into the flames.

To Moses, dusty of face, you give the way to glory; Pharaoh, the seeker of pomp, you draw into disgrace.[252]

This reversed horseshoe acts without how and why; Moses the stick-seeker, you draw into a serpent.[253]

383

Yesterday I clutched his skirt saying, "O essence [jewel] of generosity, do not say goodnight, do not grieve us, for tonight you are mine."

The darling face lit up and glowed red like a spark. He said, "That is enough; draw back. How long with this beggar's ways?"

I said, "God's Messenger said: 'Seek your need of the handsome, if you desire to attain it.'"[254]

He said, "The fair of face is self-willed and bad-tempered, for beauty permits plenty of airs and wickedness."

I said, "If that is so, his wickedness is the life of the soul, because whenever you try it, it is the talisman of the mine."

He said, "This is a raw talk; who is the handsome? This color and form is a snare, it is cunning and inconstancy.

"When a man possesses not the soul of the soul, know that he possesses not that; many a man delivers his soul with the form of mortality."

I said, "Pretty of cheek, bring nonexistence into existence; change our copper to gold, you who are the soul of alchemy.[255]

"Copper must yield itself to discover the alchemy: you are a grain of corn, but you are outside the mill."

He said, "You are ungrateful, you are ignorant of copper; you are in doubt and conjecture from the things you show."

I began crying wretchedly. I said, "You have the rule, come to the succor of your lover, O succor of light."

When he saw his servant's tears he began to laugh; East and West came to life through that grace and familiarity.

Fellow travelers and friends, weep like a cloud, so that fair ones may bring their sweet presence into the garden.

384

Once again a melody has come from the reed pipe of fortune; O soul, clap hands, O heart, stamp feet.

A mine has become aglow, a world is laughing, a table is adorned, acclamation is coming.

We are drunk and roaring in hope of the spring over the meadow, adoring one of handsome cheek.

He is the sea, we are a cloud; he the treasure, we a ruin; in the light of a sea we are as motes.

I am distracted, I am excused; suffer me to brag—with the light of Moṣṭafā I will split the moon.[256]

385

You who are weary of us, we are very desirous; you who have withdrawn from the road, where is the courtesy of fellow-traveling?

You are the marrow of the world, the rest is all hay; how shall a man get fat on eating hay?

Every city which is ruined and turned upside down, that has happened because it remained far from the royal shadow.

When the sun has gone, what remains? Black night. When reason has gone from the head, what remains but idiocy?

Reason, the riot that has befallen, all springs from your departure: and then you attribute the fault to a body without reason.

Wherever you turn your back, there is error and war; whenever you show your face, there is drunkenness and stupefaction.

The eighteen thousand worlds are of two divisions only—half

dead, inanimate matter, and half conscious.[257]

The sea of consciousness from which all minds derive, that is the goal of all finite minds.

Swimming soul, who go in this sea, and you who leap from this wheel like an arrow—

By the tent of your body a world is illuminated; so how can you be, you spirit of the tent!

Spirit, eternity is intoxicated by your wine; in your hand, earth is transmuted to pure gold;

Your description evades the understanding of the vulgar, O incompatible one, and transcends the likeness of the magnitude of one who likens you.

If any lover through yearning assigns a form to you, the sea of transcendence would not be made impure.

If the babbling poets compare the crescent moon to a horse-shoe, the moon does not lose its moonliness.

How could the sea remain a barrier in the path before Moses? And could the blind remain blind in the protection of Jesus?

He is the master of all, even if he has not one slave; that cypress of his is erect, even though you count it as not erect.

You are Moses, though still the shepherd; you are Joseph, though still in the well.

You do not receive the wages for labor because you are not always engaged in this labor, but only casually.

Silence, for without God's food and wine from the unseen these words and images are but two or three empty bowls.

386

Bird-catcher, you have set a hidden snare; over the snare you have laid smoke-colored fabric.

Too many thousands of birds you have slain by this trick and laid all the feathers plucked as a sign.

The birds that are your watchmen make a great cry; what meanings you have planted in their cries!

For the thirsty birds you have placed in the taverns of your proximity vats of Magian wines.

That vat, the scent of which neither *sāqī* nor drunkard catches, you have laid down for the sake of the nightfarer that you know.

In patience and penitence you have compounded the immunity of the shield; in cruelty and wrath you have set a lance.

Without the danger of lance and shield, you have implanted for the pious believers a kingdom in the seven oft-repeated verses.[258]

Under the black of the eye you have made the wave of light flow, and in that aged world you have set youthfulness.

In the breast which fashions forms out of imagination, you have placed a finger without pen and finger.

Though so many veils of flesh and sinew lie over the heart, you have given the heart penetration and visible passage.

Which is stranger—the glance that flies like an arrow, or the brow you have set as a bow?

Or that in vessel-like bodies you implanted various characters like wines bitter and sweet,

Or that this secret liquor distilled from the tongue you have placed on the tongue as the cream of speech?

Every essence and accident is as a mouth-shut bud which you have set as a veil over the cradle of virgins.

On the day when you cause them to blossom and remove their veils, O soul of the soul of the soul, what soul you will have implanted!

Restless hearts will see for what reason in separation you have placed entreaty and yearning.

Silence, that that soul may speak the spoken things; why have you implanted this long conjury?

387

You swore an oath that henceforth you would be cruel; now you break your oath and finish with cruelty.

Today we have seized your skirt and are drawing; how long will you offer pretexts and cheat?

Idol, that lip of yours is smiling and giving good tidings that you have resolved henceforward to be true.

Since without you entreaty is not proper for us, what profits it? It is only proper when you vouchsafe the need.

Without your sea we flounder like fish on the land—so fish do when you part them from water.

The tyrant is cruel and the prisoner terrifies him with you; God does with you what you do in our case!

When you are cruel, with whom shall anyone terrify you? Only he who submits to whatever you demand.

Silence, do not sell the unique pearl; how do you fix a price for that which is without value?

388

Reed, very sweet it is that you know the secrets; that one does the work who has knowledge of the work.

Reed, like the bolbol you are lamenting for the rose; do not scratch your neck, for you know the thornless rose.

I said to the reed, "You share the beloved's breath; do not steal the secret [from me]." The reed said, "Knowledge is for total destruction."

I said, "My salvation is in my destruction; set fire, burn, do not leave knowledge."

He said, "How shall I be a brigand on this caravan? I know that knowledge is the leader."

I said, "Since the Beloved cherished not those gone astray, knowledge has become disgusted with itself."

You who are measure of self, you have nine eyes; awareness is for us the veil of eyes and sight.[259]

You are a companion of the lip because you have been beheaded; in this way head is a shame, and knowledge a disgrace.[260]

You have become empty of self and full of secrets because you are aware of self-worshiping and unbelief.

What is lament, when you drink of the ruby of the Beloved? Let knowledge utter this bitter lament.

No, no, you do not lament of yourself, noble one; weep for him who is aware of others.

If heaven laments, the ox is under the load; you are aware of this reversed deceptive horseshoe.[261]

389

You who slay like sugar the lovers, slay my soul sweetly this moment, if you are slaying.

To slay sweetly and gently is the property of your hand, because you slay with a glance he who seeks a glance.

Every morning continuously I am waiting, waiting, because you generally slay me at dawn.

Your cruelty to us is candy; do not close the way to assistance. Is it not the case that at the end you will slay me in front of the gate?

You whose breath is without a belly, you whose sorrow repels sorrow, you who slay us in a breath like a spark,

Every moment you proffer another repulse like a shield; you have abandoned the sword and are slaying with the shield.

390

Lion-heart, you have made a hundred thousand lion-hearts; you have outstripped the sun even in generosity.

Open your eyes, and have compassion once more; break your oath, if you have sworn by God.

See that these enemies are clapping their hands, since in this rage and warlike mood you have stamped your foot.

With whom is your inclination, O soul?—so that I may become his dust, so that I may become the servant of him whom you have reckoned somebody.

Body, at last stir yourself and make an effort. Effort is blessed; why are you languid?

Rise, approach the friend; set your face to the earth, saying, "Idol sweet as sugar, by what are you vexed?"

Master of the soul, Shams-e Dīn of Tabrīzī, this head of mine is of your palm tree for it was nourished by you.

391

O soul, the breeze of spring is coming, so that you may raise your hand towards the rose garden.

Grass and lily, tulip and hyacinth said, "There grows whatever you sow."

Buds and rose blossoms came as a helmet so that the ugliness of the thorn may not appear.[262]

Elevation has come to the tall cypress, it has found glory after humiliation.

Spirit enters all the garden, for water displays spirit-bestowing;

The beauty of the garden increases from water—it has come as most blessed friendship.

Leaf has sent a message to fruit, "You come quickly, do not scratch your ear."

That sweet grape is king of the fruits, because its tree was emaciated.

In the winter of lust how long shall the garden of our heart remain imprisoned and walled in?

Seek the way from the heart, seek the moon from the soul; what does the earth possess but dust?

Rise, wash your face, but with a water which beautifies the cheek of the rose.

The branch of blossoms said to the basil, "Lay down whatever you possess in our path."

The nightingale said to the garden, "We are the quarry of your snare."

The rose entreats God for mercy, "Do not put winter in command over us."

God says, "How does juice come out of fruit until you squeeze it?

"Do not grieve over December and the raiding Ḡozz, and regard this business as lying at my door.[263]

"Thanks and praise, joy and increase do not appear except you lament.

"I will give you life unnumbered if I take away numbered life;

"I will give you wine without headache if I take away wine that yields headache."

Though many pictures have knowledge, why do you go on painting the pages?

Through you the face of the pages has been blackened; how can you read the writing of day?

Have done with smoke; look at the light from the moon of the Beloved in the dark night.

Enough, enough, come down from your horse, so that he may ride forth, the horseman supreme.

392

The Borāq of the love of realities carried away my mind and heart; ask me where it took them? Thither you do not know.[264]

I reached that arch where I saw neither moon nor sky, that world where even world is parted from world.

Give me respite for a moment for my mind to return to me; I will describe the soul to you—give ear, for you are the soul.

But approach nearer, my master, lay your ear on my mouth; for walls have ears, and this is a secret mystery.

It is a loving care from the Beloved, this so strange a grace; the lamps of vision enter by way of the ear.

Accompany the khiḍr of reason to the fountain of life, so that like the fountain of the sun by day you scatter light.[265]

As Zoleykā became young through the intention of Joseph, so the ancient world recovers its youth from this star.

The Canopus of the soul swallows moon, sun and pole of the seven skies when he rises from the Yemeni pillar.[266]

Take for a moment a clipping of faith and place it under your tongue that you may see how inwardly you are a mine of gold!

You have fallen into the mouths and men are chewing you; since you are a fine and well-baked bread, you are always the same.

You dance like a mote when light takes your hand; it is out of coldness and wetness that you are heavy as sand.

When the sun rises it says to the dark earth, "Since I became your companion, you are a master of double conjunction."[267]

You are not a goat to come and play the rearing horse; you are a shepherd like a raging lion before the herd of lions.

Light up the five lamps of your senses with the light of the heart; the senses are as the five players, the heart like the seven oft-repeated verses.

Every dawn a cry comes out of the heavens, "When you settle the dust of the road, you lead the way to a sign."

So draw not back the reins of resolution like a hermaphrodite; ahead of you are two armies toward which you advance like a lance.

Sugar has come to you, saying, "Open your mouth"; why have you closed your mouth like a pistachio to the sugar's invitation?

Take the bowl of sugar; eat by the bowlful—may you enjoy it!

Do not beat the drum of legend—why do you give in to the tongue?

Through Shams, Pride of Tabriz, you worship the sun, for he is the sun of spiritual sciences, the governor of the sun of place.

393

You are my heaven, I am the earth in astonishment; every moment what things have you set growing in my heart.

I am the dry-lipped earth; rain that water of grace. Of your water earth discovers rose and rose garden.

What does the earth know, what have you sown in its heart? It is pregnant by you, and you know what it is bearing.

Every atom is pregnant by you with another mystery; for a while you writhe with the pregnant women in agony.

What things are in the womb of this enfolded earth from which are born "I am the truth" and the cry "Glory to me!"

Now it groans, and a camel is born of its womb; a staff falls and takes the way of serpenthood.

The prophet said, "Know the believer is like a camel, always drunk with God who looks after his camel.[268]

"Now he brands him, and now sets provender before him; now he binds his knees with the shackle of reason,

"And now he loosens his knees to dance like a camel, to rend asunder the bridle and go in disarray."

See how the meadow can not contain itself for joy, since the spiritual garden has given it so many forms.

See the power of the Universal Soul to impart understanding, so that through it the dullard earth has become a spiritual shaper.

Like the Universal Soul, the whole plenum is a veil or curtain of the Sun of Majesty who has no second,

The eternal Sun which never sets, the light of whose face is neither of the Aquarius nor of Libra.

One by one all that He sowed is appearing. Silence, for the oyster shells are pregnant with the divine pearls.

394

The lord of beauty and quintessence of loveliness entered the soul and mind as a man will stroll in the garden at spring.

Come, come, for you are the life and salvation of men; come, come, for you are the eye and lamp of Joseph.

Lay foot on my water and clay, for through your foot darkness and veiledness depart from water and clay.

Through your glow stones turn to rubies, through your searching the searcher reaches his goal.

Come, come, for you bestow beauty and glory; come, come, for you are the cure of a thousand Jacobs.

Come, come, though you have never departed, but I speak every word to you for a desired end.

Sit in the place of my soul, for you are a thousand times my soul; slay your paramour and lover, for you are the Beloved.

If the king is not the king of the world, O melancholy world, by His life I bid you say, "Why are you in confusion?"

Now you are gay and fresh with His green banner, and now you are overtuned by the heart of His army of battle.

Now, like the thought of an artist, you fashion forms; now you sweep carpets like the broom of the porter.

When you sweep a form, you give its quintessence angelhood, and the wings and pinions of the cherubim.

Silence, guard the water strictly like a waterbag, for if you sprinkle it through a crack, know that you are at fault.

Your heart has reached Shams, the Pride of Tabriz, because the Doldol of the heart proved itself a nimble mount.[269]

395

Finally you have broken away and departed into the Unseen; I wonder, I wonder—by which way did you depart from the world?

You beat your feathers and wings mightily and broke your cage; you took the air and departed towards the spiritual world.

You were a special falcon in captivity to an old woman; when you heard the falcon-drum, you departed to the placeless.[270]

You were a drunken nightingale amongst owls; the scent of the rose garden arrived, you departed to the rose garden.

You suffered much crop sickness from this sour ferment; finally you departed to the eternal tavern.

You went straight as an arrow to the target of bliss; you flew to that target and departed from this bow.

This world like a ghoul gave you false clues; you took no heed of the clue and departed to the clueless.

Since you have become the sun, what have you to do with a crown? Since you have departed from the middle, why do you seek a belt?

I have heard tell of gazing on the soul when the eyes are extinguished; why do you gaze on the soul, since you have departed to the soul of soul?

O heart, what a rare bird you are, that in hunting for the All-Grateful you departed towards the lance with two wings like a shield.[271]

The rose flees from autumn; ah, what a bold rose you are, that you went creeping along before the autumn wind.

Like rain from heaven on the roof of the earthly world you ran in every direction and departed by the spout.

Be silent, suffer not the anguish of speech; sleep on, for you have departed into the shelter of such a loving friend.

396

Come, come, for you will not find another friend like me; where indeed in both worlds is a beloved like me?

Come, come, and do not pass your days in every direction, for there is no other market elsewhere for your money.

You are like a dry water conduit and I am like the rain; you are like a ruined city and I am like the architect.

Except in serving me, which is the sunrise of joy, men have never seen and never will see any mark of happiness.

In sleep you see a thousand moving forms; when sleep has gone, you see not a single creature.[272]

Close the eye of wrong and open the eye of intelligence, for the carnal soul has fallen like an ass, and concupiscence is the halter.[273]

Seek sweet syrup from the garden of love, for human nature is a vinegar-seller and a crusher of unripe grapes.

Come to the hospital of your Creator, for no sick man can do without that physician.

The world without that king is like the body without its head; wind round such a head as a turban.

If you are not black, let not the mirror go from your hand; for the soul is your mirror and the body is rust.[274]

Where is the lucky merchant with Jupiter in ascension, that I may do that business with him and purchase his goods?[275]

Come, think of me who gave you thought; if you are buying rubies, at least buy from my mine.

Go on foot towards him who gave you a foot, gaze on him with both eyes who gave you sight.

Clap hands for joy for him from whose sea is the foam, for there is no grief or sorrow happening to him.

Listen without ears; speak unto him without a tongue, for the speech of the tongue is not without contradiction and injury.

397

If you have no beloved, why do you not seek one? And if you have attained the Beloved, why do you not rejoice?

If the companion is not complaint, why do you not become him? If the rebec wails not, why do you not teach it manners?

If an Abū Jahl is a veil to you, why do you not attack Abū Jahl and Abū Lahab?

You sit idly saying, "This is a strange business"; you are the strange one not to desire such a strange one.

You are the sun of the world; why are you black at heart? See that you do not any more have a desire for the knot [of Draco].[276]

Like gold you are prisoner in the furnace so that you may not be covetous of the purse of gold.[277]

Since Unity is the bachelor's chamber of those who say "One," why do you not make your spirit a bachelor to all but God?

Have you ever seen Majnūn have affection with two Leylīs? Why not desire only one face and one chin?

There is such a moon in hiding in the night of your being; why do you not pray and petition at midnight?

Though you are an ancient drunkard and not new to the wine, God's wine does not suffer you not to make turmoil.

My wine is the fire of love, especially from the hand of God; may life be unlawful to you, since you do not make your life firewood.

Though the wave of discourse is surging, yet it is better that you should expound it with heart and soul, not with lips.

398

Heart, you are the phoenix of union. Fly, why do you not fly? No one recognizes you, neither man nor peri.

You are the sweetheart, not the heart; but with every device and trickery you have taken the shape of the heart so that you will ravish a thousand hearts.

For a moment faithfully you mingle with earth, and for a moment you pass beyond empyrean and firmament and the bounds of the two worlds.

Why does not spirit find you, for you are its wings and feathers? Why does not sight see you who are the source of sight?

What fear has penitence to repent of you? What is consciousness that it should remain conscious along with you?

What shall be that poor copper when the alchemy comes? Will it not pass away from copperhood into the attribute of gold?

Who is that poor seed when the springtime comes? Does not its seedhood pass away into treehood?

Who is poor brushwood when it falls into the fire? Is not the brushwood transformed into a spark by the flame?

All reason and science are stars; are you the sun of the world who tear asunder their veils?

The world is like snow and ice, and you are the season of summer; when you, king, are on its track, no trace of it remains.

Say, who am I to remain along with you? I and a hundred like me will pass away when you gaze towards me.

The perfection of the description of the lord Shams-e Tabrīzī surpasses the imaginations of predestinator and free-willer.

399

We have come once again to a lord to whose knee no sea reaches.

Tie together a thousand minds, they will not reach Him; how shall a hand or foot reach the moon in heaven?

The sky stretched out its throat eagerly to Him; it found no kiss, but it swallowed a sweetmeat.

A thousand throats and gullets stretched towards His lip. "Scatter too on our heads manna and quails."

We have come again to a Beloved, from whose air a shout has reached our ears.

We have come again to that sanctuary to bow the brow which is to surpass the skies.

We have come again to that meadow to whose bolbol *'anqā* is a slave.[278]

We have come to Him who was never apart from us; for the waterbag is never filled without the existence of a water-carrier.

The bag always clings to the body of the water-carrier, saying, "Without you, I have no hand or knowledge or opinion."

We have come again to that feast with the sweet dessert of which the sugarcane chewer attained his desire.

We have come again to that sphere, in whose bent the soul roars like thunder.

We have come again to that love at whose contact the *dīv* has become peri-like.

Silence! Seal the rest under your tongue, for a jealous tutor has been put in charge of you.

Speak not of the talk of the Pride of Tabriz, Shams-e Dīn, for the rational mind is not suitable for that speech.

400

Leap, leap from the world, that you may be king of the world; seize the sugar tray that you may be a sugar plantation.

Leap, leap like a meteor to slay the *dīv*; when you leap out of stardom, you will be the pole of heaven.[279]

When Noah sets out for the sea, you will be his ship; when the Messiah goes to heaven, you will be the ladder.

Now like Jesus of Mary you become the soul's physician; and now like Moses of 'Emran you will go forth to be a shepherd.

There is a spiritual fire for the sake of cooking you; if you leap back like a woman, you will be a raw cuckold.

If you do not flee from the fire, and become wholly cooked like well-baked bread, you will be a master and lord of the table.

When you come to the table and the brethren receive you, like bread you will be sustenance of the soul and you will be the soul.

Though you are the mine of pain, by patience you will become the treasure; though you are a flawed house, you will be a knower of the unseen.

I said this, and a call came from heaven to my spirit's ear saying, "If you become like this, you will be like that."

Silence! the mouth is intended for cracking sugar, not for you to cast slack and become a chin-wagger.

Notes

201

F 1623

[1]The literal translation of the line would be: "It was all my fault that such an art came forth from me: I purposely drew a scorpion toward my own foot."

Aflākī writes: "There was an assembly for a great *samā'* in the house of Parvāna. Mowlānā was in a great ecstasy, but Seyyed Sharaf al-dīn and Parvāna had retired to a corner and were reproaching him. Mowlānā heard them and composed this *ğazal* . . . Parvāna immediately apologized and did not give Sharaf al-dīn such an occasion any more." *Manāqeb*, 339–40.

202

F 1628

[2]Solomon had dominion over men, Jinns, and birds, and he had a magic seal with which he exercised his influence.

203

F 1634

204

F 1638

[3]In the original: *faraḥ ebn faraḥ ebn faraḥ ebn faraḥām*. For the sake of the introduction or induction of a certain rhythmic mood Rūmī often bursts into a repetition of a single word or phrase.

[4]The Garden of Eram was the famous garden built by Shaddād in Arabia Felix, see *E.I* 2: 519.

[5]Ḥātem was an Arab chief whose generosity is proverbial.

205

F 1641

206

F 1649

[6]The Wailing Column was in the Prophet's mosque at Medina. According to tradition it moaned when he grasped it. See note 6 to 62 in vol. 1; also Nicholson on *Math.* 1:2113.

207

F 1655

[7]In Persian literature indigo and black are two colors of mourning.

[8]For Abraham see *First Selection*, note 6 to 8.
Ebrāhīm son of Adham (d. 783?) was a famous Sufi from Balk whose life story strangely resembles that of Buddha.

[9]*Rūmī* (Roman) is white-skinned, while Zangī is dark-skinned. They also stand for day and night respectively, and are in turn associated with happiness and grief.

[10]This is somewhat different from Arberry's original translation. Literally: "Your soul is unanchored (i.e., insecure) as is your dust-filled body." Arberry's version was: "Like the body of your earth-sack on the top of the water of your soul, the soul is veiled in the body alike in wedding feast or sorrow."

[11]Zamazm: a well in Mecca.

208

F 1663

[12]The Companion of the Cave is Abū Bakr who accompanied the Prophet in his flight from Mecca. They stayed three days in a cave outside Mecca on their way to Medina. The Qur'an refers to the incident in sura 9: 40: "If you do not help him, yet God has helped him already, when the unbelievers drove him forth, the second of the two; when the two were in the cave, when he said to his companion, 'Sorrow not; surely God is with us.'"

209

F 1678

[13]Abu'l Ḥikam (Father of Wisdom) was the title of 'Amr Ebn Hešām, one of the most bitter enemies of the Prophet, who was killed in the second year of the Hejra (624) in the battle of Badr. Moḥammad nicknamed him Abū Jahl (Father of Ignorance) because of his uncompromising attitude towards Islam. Cf. Nicholson's notes on *Math.* 1: 782, 1503.

210

F 1688

[14]To experience divine love is a spiritual regeneration or birth for a Sufi. This is why the soul in the world is compared to the embryo in the womb, and when it becomes a babe just born into a new world. Cf. *Math.* notes, 1: 19, 3180. Rūmī says that such a love was inborn in him and from the beginning he embarked on his Sufi mission.

"On that" refers to that love. It was a common superstition that if, while cutting the umbilical cord, one made a wish the child would attain it.

[15]*Lawḥ-e ḡayb* (the Unseen Tablet) seems to be the same as *lawḥ-e maḥfūz* (the Preserved Tablet, Qur'an, 85: 22) which refers to the Qur'an. It is said to have been in heaven before its revelation. The Sufis interpret it as the First Intelligence (*'aql-e avval*) or Logos or the Active Intellect (*'aql-e fa'āl*). See Sajjādī, *Farhang-e 'erfānī*, 405, and Nicholson's note on *Math.* 1: 296.

[16]Covenant of Alast: *Alastu bi rabbikum?*, "Am I not your Lord?" (Qur'an 7: 171). Thus God addressed the future generations of men (according to the Sufis their souls). They answered "Yes," and acknowledged God's right to judge their actions and to punish their sins.

211

F 1690, N 37

[17]Abū Lahab was the unconvinced pagan uncle of Moḥammad. In 616 when the pagans decided to boycott the Prophet and his friends, Abū Lahab, who was of the Quraish, withdrew his protection from his nephew. Cf. Qur'an III.

[18]The finest quality glass was produced in Aleppo.

[19]Baṣra was well-known for its dates. Rūmī says that without the Baṣra of your being (i.e., without Shams) he would not have tasted a date (i.e., spiritual experience).

212

F 1692

213

F 1705

[20]Aḥmad is the title of Moḥammad.

[21]"The believer is prudent, sagacious and cautious," *Aḥādīs*, 67.

214

F 1713

[22]"Street of mourning": the world, which has been called by many similar names, such as "the infidel's paradise," and symbolized by the false dawn, a carcass, a bath-stove and a tomb. (Cf. "world" in Nicholson's index to *Math.*).

215

F 1725

[23]According to Aflākī Sultan Rokn-al-dīn, Saljūqī was invited to Āq Sarāi by his emirs to decide about the strategy to face the approaching Mongol horde. He consulted Mowlānā, who said: "It is better not to go there." But Rokn-al-dīn went and was strangled by his own people. It is reported that before his death, he shouted: "Mowlānā, Mowlānā!" Meanwhile Rūmī was at *Semā'*. He told the disciples of Rokn-al-dīn's death and composed this poem. *Manāqeb* 1: 147–8.

216

F 1737

[24]Ḥabīb Najjār (Carpenter) is a legendary character who gave his name to a shrine below mount Silpuis at Anṭakiya. Though not mentioned by name in the Qur'an (36: 12ff), Muslim tradition finds him there under the description of a man who was put to death in a village for urging the villagers not to reject the three apostles who had come with the divine message. Some scholars have suggested that Ḥabīb is the Agabus of *Acts*, II: 28, but there is not enough evidence to substantiate this suggestion. Cf G. Vajda's article in *E.I.*

217

F 1739
[25]A *ḥadīs* attributed to Moḥammad says: "The true believer resembles a lute whose voice will not improve unless its belly is empty." *Aḥādīs*, 222.

218

F 1754
[26]In Persian poetry the abode of Jesus after his ascension is usually said to be in the Fourth Heaven (the sphere of the sun), although Ebn al-'Arabī *(Fotūḥāt)* places him in the Second Heaven. See *Math.* 1: 649.

219

F 1760
[27]According to Aflākī *(Manāqeb*, 703), this *ğazal* is the fourth letter in verse sent by Rūmī to Shams-e Tabrīzī during the latter's journey to Syria.
[28]In the original, Rūmī plays on the two meanings of *šām* (i.e., evening and Syria).

220

F 1769
[29]*Nūn wa'l-qalam* is the beginning of sura 68. Sufis interpret *nūn* as Divine Knowledge and *al-qalam* as the Universal Reason (or *'aql-e avval).* Cf. *Math.* notes, 5: 1964.
[30]This line is not clear in Arberry's handwritten translation. A more literal translation is "like a strange Arabic word in Persian."
[31]The second hemistich of this line is from a poem by the Arab poet, al-A'shā, who speaking of wine, says: "And exposed it to the wind, in its jar, and he praised its jar, (and petitioned for it that it might not become sour nor spoil)." See Lane's *Lexicon* under *irtisām.*

221

F 1786
[32]"Seven heavens" refers to the spheres of the seven planets. According to ancient Oriental geography the seas or oceans of the earth were also seven in number.
[33]For "Joseph of Canaan," see *First Selection,* note 1 to 7.
[34]The Water of Life *(Ab-e ḥayvān* or *ḥayāt)* is the Fountain of Life in the Land of Darkness. Niẓāmī in his *Sikandar-nāma* describes how Alexander was guided by the prophet Khidr to the Fountain but could not reach it. See *First Selection,* note on 6, verse 2.
[35]Color and scent are symbols for the world of phenomena; see *First Selection,* note on 71, verse 5, and Nicholson on *Math.* 1: 1121–35.
[36]Bodies are composed of the four elements: earth, water, fire, and air. All these originally come from God.
[37]For Ṣalāḥ-al-dīn Zarkūb, see *First Selection,* note on 29, verse 12.

222

F 1789, N 36
[38]Nicholson in his translation of this *ğazal (Selected Poems from the Dīvāni Shamsī Tabrīz*, 36) compares the image of "the inverted candles" with the line in Shakespeare's Sonnet XXI: "those gold candles fixed in heaven's air."
[39]Nicholson illustrates the idea with a line from *Gulshan-i Rāz*, 165:
Each atom doth invisibly enshrine
The deep-veil'd beauty of the Soul divine.

223

F 1794
[40]"Do not despair of God's mercy," Qur'an, 39: 53.
[41]For the angel Seraphiel, see *First Selection*, note on 71, verse 3.
In the pre-Islamic Iran *Mehragān* (autumn festival in honor of Mithra) was as important as *Naw-rūz*, the beginning of the Persian calendar in the spring.
[42]Indians as well as black people symbolize the night.

224

F 1807
[43]*Doš* and *qoš* are imperative forms from the modern Turkish *duşmak* and *koşmak* respectively. The latter could be read as *Kaş* (run away) instead of *Koş* (set off). Mowlānā occasionally used Turkish words and sometimes wrote *ğazals* in Anatolian Turkish. On his Turkish poetry, see Serefeddin Yaltkaya, "Mevlâna da Türkçe kelimelar va Türkçe siirler," *Turkiyat Mecmuasi* (1934), 112–68; Mecdut Mansuroglu, "Celaluddin Rumi's Turkish verse" in *Ural-altaische Jahrbücher* 24 (1952), 106–15.

225

F 1823
[44]For "the water of life," see note 34.
The reflection of the moon in the well is likened to Joseph cast by his brothers into a dark well. Cf. Qur'an 12.
[45]*Samā'*, which here has been translated as "concert," is the mystic dance of the Mevlevi darvishes accompanied by the flute and the recital of *ğazals*. The musical quality of most of the poems in the *Dīvān-e Shams* makes them ideal for such performances, and apparently Rūmī had this particular point in mind when he wrote them (cf. p. 3 in the introduction to the *First Selection).* Here Rūmī opposed those Sufis and orthodox Muslims who were against the *samā'* as a ritual. There have been numerous pro and con discussions on the subject in Islamic literature, and for instance one can refer to al-Ğazālī *(Kīmīyā-ye Sa'ādat,* Tehran, 1954, chap. 15) who considers the charms of music of great help in drawing the sensitive heart toward God.

226

F 1826

[46]Perhaps Rūmī refers to the Qur'an where it says: "He [God] sends down His angels with inspiration of His command, to such of His servants as He pleases," 16: 2.

[47]"The black and blue chest" is the sign of asceticism and the chastised carnal soul *(nafs)* without whose abasement the Sufi will not attain any spiritual elevation.

[48]"Hū" or "Yā Hū" are the ecstatic cries of the Sufis and mean "He" [God] or "O God!" The scent of the Beloved from His divine city is likened to the perfume of Joseph's vest which, coming from afar to the blind Jacob, gave him his sight. Cf. Qur'an 12: 94.

227

F 1837

[49]Arberry's translation was: "you are . . . my only one and my thousand times."

[50]"The house of water and clay" symbolizes the human body where the soul, coming from a spiritual land, must sojourn and the original abode back to which it wishes to fly.

228

F 1845

[51]Moses' face was illuminated by divine glory. One of the signs of his prophethood was his White Hand (yadd-e bayḍā). See Qur'an 7: 105 *et seq.).* 'Emrān was the father of Moses.

[52]Hāmān was the minister of Pharaoh (Qur'an 28: 6).

[53]Another sign of Moses' prophethood was his rod which changed into a serpent (Qur'an 7: 108).

[54]For Abū Horaira's magic bag, see *First Selection*, note 10 to 157, and *Math.* 5: 2794.

[55]After casting Joseph into the well, they told Jacob that he had been eaten by a wolf. For Bū Jahl, see note 13.

[56]The hatred of the black beetle for sweet scents is proverbial.

[57]The reference is to a tradition which says: "Consult women and do the opposite," *Aḥādīs*, 30.

[58]Qibla is the direction of Kaaba towards which the Muslims turn their faces while praying.

[59]Arberry's translation was: "it fills from its lip with sweets from the floor of the house to the attic."

[60]Qur'an 54: 55.

229

F 1850

[61]"And the earth—We spread it forth." Qur'an 51: 48. *Farrāš* is a servant.

[62]Abraham: see *First Selection*, note on 8, verse 6.

[63]A *ḥadīs* attributed to Moḥammad *(Jāme'-e Ṣaḡīr,* 2: 49); F 4: 140.

230

F 1861

231

F 1869
[64]For Khidr, see note 34.

232

F 1876
[65]The clay of man was imbued with divine wine before his creation and this symbolizes the love of God.
[66]Names: ninety-nine beautiful names of God (Qur'an 7: 180).
[67]Rūmī is playing with the words which occur in the Muslim profession of faith: *lā ilāha illā 'llāh* (there is no God but *Allāh*). *Illā* is used in antithesis to *lā*. In order to reach the kingdom of *illā* (or real existence in God) one has to undergo the Sufi experience of self-annihilation.
[68]Majnūn, which literally means elf-ridden or madly in love, is the proverbial lover in Islamic literatures.
[69]The Christians under Muslim rule were required to carry a distinctive girdle *(zonnār)*.
[70]For Khidr, see note 34.

233

F 1888

234

F 1898
[71]"(O soul) return to thy Lord, well-pleased and well-pleasing." Qur'an 89: 28.
[72]Māčīn: the lands beyond China.
[73]The family of Yāsīn: the family of Moḥammad.

235

F 1904
[74]"The Companions of the Elephant" were the army of the Abyssinian Abraha who attacked Mecca in AD 571, See Qur'an 105, and *First Selection*, note on 126, verse 13.
[75]According to the Qur'an 105, God sent large flights of birds called *abābīl* to fling stones at the army of Abraha and destroy it.

236

F 1910

237

F 1919, N 35.

[76]Nicholson's version is: *mar dīde-ye ḵwīsh rā nadīdan*—(not to see your own eye) "whence all objects derive their unreal existence."

238

F 1925
[77]Loqmān seems to be Aesop in Islamic tradition. Nicholson writes: "He appears as a sagacious negro slave in several anecdotes related by Rūmī. One of these *[Math.* 1: 3584 *et seq.]* is identical with a story which occurs in the fourteenth-century *Life of Aesop* by Maximus Planudes." *Math.* 1: 1961.

239

F 1937
[78]Any object which keeps one from being absorbed in divine love is an idol.
[79]See Nicholson's commentary on 1: 400-1.
[80]*Ḵiyāl* (fantasy or phantasm) is the same as the World of Similitude *('ālam-e meṣāl),* of which everything in the sensible world *('ālam-e šahāda)* is a reflection. The World of Similitude is a purgatory stage between the worlds of souls and things." Sajjādī *Farhang-e 'erfānī,* 204.

240

F 1947
[81]According to Nicholson *(Math.* 1: 2778) Ja'farī gold refers to the gold produced by the Shi'ite Imam, Ja'far-al-Ṣādeq, who was the reputed author of several works on alchemy. Also, it has been said that Hārūn-al-Rashīd entrusted the coinage in Islamic domains to Ja'far the Barmecide and hence the name. In both cases it refers to pure gold.
[82]Rūmī plays on the two meanings of *māh* (moon and month). Thus the line also means: the festival of everyone is the time of the year (or the month) of which he is fond.
[83]Qur'an 24: 35: "God is the Light of the heavens and the earth . . ." which is "neither of the East nor of the West."

241

F 1957

242

F 1958
[84]"Oil": sauce or gravy.

243

F 1965

[85]Āzar: the father of Abraham was a famous idol-maker. Mānī, the founder of Manichaean religion, is said to have been a great painter.

244

F 1972

[86]For the comparison of the heart to a pond fed by streams, see Nicholson on *Math.* 1: 2710–14.

[87]Guebre: a Zoroastrian.

[88]*Ḳomār* (intoxicated, hazy or languid look) is used by Persian poets to describe the beautiful eyes of their beloved.

[89]Water and clay: man's body, which is a cage for his soul.

[90]Qur'an 30: 72.

245

F 1983

[91]*Talqīn* is part of the funeral ceremony in which the Muslim profession of faith is recited to the dead.

246

F 1986

[92]For Joseph and the women of Egypt, see Qur'an 12: 31, and *First Selection*, note on 7, verse 1.

[93]God "created man out of a clot of congealed blood." Qur'an 96: 2.

[94]Water and clay: the human body. The Abode of War: the world.

247

F 2000

[95]Referring to the well-known saying: "Everything returns to its origin."

[96]The Ocean (in the original, *Qolzom*) of Light symbolizes spiritual truth, since "God is the Light of the heavens and the earth" (Qur'an 24: 35).

[97]The reference is to the epiphany *(tajallī)* of God on Mount Sinai, which shattered the mountain and left Moses in a swoon.

248

F 2003

[98]Ḳotan: Chinese Turkestan which was proverbially known for its beautiful inhabitants.

[99]Scattering coins over the head of the bride is still done in the East.

[100]Jacob smelled from afar the perfume of Joseph's vest (Qur'an 12: 94).

249

F 2006

Notes

[101]*Fāteḥa*, the first sura of the Qur'an, is recited several times in daily prayers. Bu'l-Fotāḥ seems to be a *konya* or title meaning "father of victories." Golpinarli, following the same idea, translates the line: "If you recite *Fāteḥa* over a grave, the person will rise with the victorious ones. . ." (4: 249). Otherwise, one might think that the reference is to Abu'l Fotūḥ Rāżī, the celebrated commentator of the Qur'an, meaning a man like Abu'l Fotūḥ rises when the *fāteḥa* is recited.

250

F 2010

[102]Any obstacle which keeps the lover away from the divine beloved is designated as a veil.

[103]"And We taught him the knowledge from Us," Qur'an 18: 65.

[104]Beginning of the sura 140.

251

F 2015

[105]. Moḥammad said: "I take refuge from poverty in You (i.e., God)," and also: "My poverty is my pride." These two seemingly contradictory statements are explained by the Sufis as pertaining to two types of poverty. One which comes close to heresy is the poverty of heart, taking away from it learning, morality, patience, submission and trust in God. The other type makes man devoid of all worldly attachments for the sake of God and is a spiritual self-surrender and self-annihilation. Such poverty is the first step in Sufism. See Sajjādī's *Farhang-e 'erfānī*, 363-6, and Ghanī's *Baḥs dar āṣār va afkār va aḥvāl-e Ḥāfiẓ*, 275 *et seq.*

[106]In the past rings were inserted in the ears of slaves as a sign of servitude.

252

F 2028

253

F 2039

[107]According to Aflākī *(Manāqeb,* 589–90) this was the last poem Rūmī composed on his death bed. His son, Bahā'-al-dīn, was with him and unable to sleep and so his dying father began this *ġazal* in order to console him and make him go to bed.

For another translation of this poem, see P. Avery, "Jalāl ud-Dīn Rūmī and Shams-i-Tabrīzī with Certain Problems in Translation," *The Muslim World* 46 (July 1956), 3: 250-2.

[108]It is believed that the emerald has the property of blinding serpents; see Nicholson's *Commentary* on *Math.* 3: 2548.

[109]Bū 'Alī is Abu 'Alī Ebn Sīnā (Avicenna) (d. 1037) and Bu'l-'Alā (d. 1057) is the famous Syrian philosopher and poet. Avery in his notes to the poem writes: "Bu'l-'Alā was used by Mowlānā to mean 'so-and-so'"; see Nicholson's *Commentary* on *Math.* 3: 776, "a *konya* bestowed ironically on any foolish boaster."

156

'Bū 'Alī (Ebn Sīnā) did not write a *History*, but he did write a book in the title of which *Tanbīh* was a component. Rūmī deliberately transposes the two.

254

F 2043
[110]When Abraham was cast into the fire, God said: "O fire, be thou cool, and a safety for Abraham." Qur'an 21: 69.
[111]Hamza ebn 'Abd-al-Moṭṭaleb, the Prophet's uncle, was a dauntless warrior and called the "Lion of God" by Moḥammad.

255

F 2053
[112]Qur'an 1: 5.
[113]The red sunset color is likened to the color of henna.

256

F 2054, N 37
[114]God is foreign to the world, yet never absent from it, i.e., He at once transcends and pervades all phenomenal existence. Cf. *Nafaḥāt al-Ons*, 183, 1.2 (Nicholson's note).
[115]After this line, Nicholson's version has an extra line which is not in F.

257

F 2061
[116]The Turks were well known for their beauty and cruelty. *Chelebi* in Turkish means "sir."

258

F 2071

259

F 2076

260

F 2083

261

F 2091

262

F 2092

[117]Kowsar is a river in paradise.

[118]Haydar (lion) was a nickname given to the Caliph 'Alī.

[119]Gorjīs was a prophet who according to the Islamic traditions was slain seventy times by his people and again came to life.

263

F 2105

[120]Perhaps a better translation would be: "With you it becomes the resident of the best tranquillity."

264

F 2107

265

F 2110

266

F 2117

267

F 2120

[121]According to the Qur'an (34: 10-11) David was a skillful maker of coats of mail.

[122]Abraham asked God to show him the dead come to life. God ordered him to take four birds and cut them into pieces and place them on every hill. When Abraham called to them, the birds came to life and flew to him from every corner (Qur'an 2: 62).

[123]The rest of the poem is in Arabic.

268

F 2130

[124]"When We said to the angels: 'Bow down before Adam.' They all bowed except Eblīs." Qur'an 2: 33.

Hindu: slave or servant.

[125]For qibla see note 59.

[126]*Hā* and *hū* are two onomatopoetics used in calling a person. The latter could be associated with the ecstatic cries of the Sufis "Hū" (God, or He is). See note 49.

269

F 2135

[127]During his ascension Moḥammad saw four streams near the *sidra* two of which were hidden and two of which were flowing openly. According to Gabriel the latter ones were the Nile and Euphrates and the other ones were two of the streams of paradise. See Golpinarli, 1: 439.

[128]This is a more literal translation than Arberry's. The original translation was: "How long will you respite me?"

270

F 2142

[129]Masjed-e Aqsā is a mosque in Jerusalem.

271

F 2144

[130]*Ham dil o ham dast* means an associate and confidant. Arberry's translation is "my fellow in heart and hand."

[131]The last part of the last line was revised. The original translation was: "What has your ecstasy to do with speech?"

272

F 2155

[132]"O you who believe! Fear God as He should be feared, and die not except in a state of Islam." Qur'an 3: 102.

273

F 2157

274

F 2166

275

F 2170

276

F 2172

[133]"And He is with you wheresoever you may be." Qur'an 57: 4.

[134]"We are nearer to him (i.e., to man) than his jugular vein." Qur'an 1: 16.

277

F 2180

[135]The Abode of Security seems to be an allusion to heaven which is sometimes called "the abode of peace" *(dār-al-salām)* by Rūmī as against "the abode of pride" *(dār-al-ğorūr)* i.e., the world. According to some commentaries in Rūmī's time Bokhara was also called *dar-al-salām*. See Gowharīn 4: 383–4.

[136]*Ṣāheb qerān* is a person who is born under a happy conjunction of the planets.

278

F 2195

279

F 2205

[137]*Qabqābs* are wooden shoes. This term is still used in Lebanon for slippers. See F 7: 387.

[138]Kay-Qobād was the second king of the legendary Kayānid dynasty. Sultan Sanjar was a Saljuq king who ruled over Iran from 1117 to 1157. Sohrāb was one of the heroes in the *Shāhnāma*.

[139]*Faqīh*, a theologian.

[140]Ebn Bawwāb (d. 1031) was a chamberlain to the Caliph al-Ma'mūn and a famous calligrapher who wrote in *reqā'* style. Rūmī puns on Ebn Bawwāb and *bawwāb* (the Doorkeeper), and on *reqā'* and *roq'a* (a letter).

[141]Qāżi is a judge.

280

F 2114, N 38

[142]A different translation of this *ğazal* is given by Arberry in his *Classical Persian Literature*, 220–1.

281

F 2226

[143]The expression comes from a legend about the creation of the cat. The animals in the Ark of Noah complained of the mouse which was eating and destroying everything. So God ordered the lion to sneeze and the cat came out from his nose. *Ḥayāt al-Ḥayvān*, 1: 17 (quoted by Forūzānfar in 7: 372).

282

F 2232

[144]For the water of life see note 34.

283

F 2239, N 39

[145]"(O soul) return to your Lord, well-pleased and well-pleasing." Qur'an 89: 28.
[145]*Sar-e Kar* was translated by Arberry as "donkeyhead" and has been changed into "meddler." *Sar-ekar* is someone who causes embarrassment, before whom one cannot talk openly.

284

F 2244

285

F 2253
[147]*'Arafa* is the ninth of *Zo'l Hejja.*

286

F 2259
[149]The reference is to this verse of the Qur'an: "Then He comprehended in His design the sky, and it had been as smoke." (41: 11).

287

F 2266
[149]The reference might be to the *hadīs* which says: "Fasting in the winter is a gain in the cold." See Ebn Aṣir, *al-Nahāya fī garīb al-hadīs wa al-aṣar,* 3: 390.
[150]I could not find this particular tradition, but there are a number of *hadīs* which bear resemblance to this. Two of them are: "Fast when you see the moon and break your fast when you see it again," and "Then fast until you see the crescent of the moon." See A. J. Wensinck, *Concordance et indices de la tradition musulmane,* Leiden, 1955, 3: 454.
[151]See Motanabbī, *Dīvān,* Beirut, 1964, 101.

288

F 2277
[152]Kay-kosrow was one of the ancient kings of Iran.

289

F 2280

290

F 2283

291

F 2293
 [153]To scratch the back of one's neck or ear signifies embarrassment.

292

F 2299
 [154]Qur'an 12: 26.

293

F 2303

294

F 2313

295

F 2319
 [155]The Brethren of Purity (apart from its literal meaning) refers to a secret society which was formed in the eighth century to introduce Greek philosophy to the Muslim world. The treatises written by them are called *Rasā'el-e Ekvān al-Ṣafā*.

296

F 2322
 [156]Aflākī gives the following account of the composition of this *ğazal*: "A darvish asked Mowlānā: 'Who is a mystic?' He said 'A mystic is a person whose calm disposition is never disturbed by any annoyance. The mystic never becomes angry.'" *Manāqeb*, 279.

297

F 2331

298

F 2335

299

F 2336

300

F 2345

301

F 2357
[157]Lines ten, eleven and twelve are in Arabic.

302

F 2370

303

F 2372

304

F 2379

305

F 2389, N 40
[158]According to Nicholson *(Dīvān-i Shams,* 238, 300) this is a reference to the *ḥadīṣ* of the Prophet, where God says: "My earth and heaven contain me not, but the heart of my believing servant contains me."
[159]"He is the Truth," Qur'an 22: 6.
[160]Reason is annihilated in mystical love.
[161]For Ṣalāḥ-al-dīn Zarkūb see *First Selection,* note to 29.

306

F 2395, N 41
[162]The air of Iraq is a Persian tune.

307

F 2399
[163]Islamic writers regarded the liver as the seat of the passion and anguish of love. The liver being on fire means that the lover is tormented by the fire of love.

308

F 2405
[164]For *Lā ilāha illa 'llāh* see note 68.

309

F 2412

[165]Turks were well known for their beauty and also for mistreatment of their lovers. A Persian-Turk seems to be a Turk born in Iran.

[166]Hasanak is a common name for boys. Here it simply means "the boy."

310

F 2422

311

F 2429

[167]Qur'an 9: 111.

[168]Qur'an 2: 151.

312

F 2437

[169]In Persian the expression "to clutch someone's skirt" means to seek his protection or help.

[170]Qur'an 6: 11.

[171]*Raml* (sand divination) was a method of divination used in the past. It made use of a board divided into sixteen sections with words on each section; these were then divided into four major parts according to the four elements. The divination would be made by throwing grains of sand on the board and basing the prediction upon their respective situations on it.

313

F 2449

[172]For Āzar see note 86.

[173]The love of Leylī and Majnūn is proverbial in Islamic literatures.

314

F 2458

315

F 2465

[174]For qibla see note 59.

[175]"Say your prayers and give charity and lend God a good loan." Qur'an 73: 20.

[176]"O you believers! Fear God and give up what remains of your demand for usury, if you are indeed believers." Qur'an 2: 278.

316

F 2474

317

F 2480
[177]Arberry's translation of this line is: "What have you seen in the courtyard? Why are you flying to annihilation?" In fact *fanā* has two meanings in Arabic, "nothingness" and a "courtyard," but it may be more appropriate to interpret both words as meaning "nothingness" or "annihilation."
[178]Moses said to the Samaritan: "Be gone! But they punishment in this life will be that thou wilt say, 'Touch me not.'" Qur'an 20: 97.

318

F 2491

319

F 2493

320

F 2498
[179]*Owtād* (props or pegs) are the saints who are believed to be the guardians and preservers of the world. Nicholson writes in his notes to the *Math.* 2: 1935: "It is well known among Sufis that every night the *Autād* must go round the whole world, and if there should be any place on which their eyes have not fallen, next day some imperfection will appear; and they must then inform the *Quṭb*, in order that he may fix his attention on the weak spot, and that by his blessing the imperfection be removed."
[180]'Anqā or Sīmorğ is the legendary bird by which the Sufis sometimes represent the unknown God. Sīmorğ is sometimes considered to symbolize the perfect man.
[181]*Evn-al-vaqt*, literally "the son of the moment."
[182]"Come back thou to thy Lord, well-pleased [thyself], and well-pleasing unto Him." Qur'an 80: 89.
[183]To bite one's hand is a sign of regret.
[184]Arberry had translated *markab* as "horse," but "ship" seems more appropriate in this context.

321

F 2509
[185]It is said that Solomon had power over the *dīvs* and jinns, see note 20.
[186]Qur'an 21: 93.

322

F 2514

323

F 2523
187Perhaps a better reading is "who burns like sulphur in a fire."

324

F 2530

325

F 2537

326

F2546

327

F 2558

328

F 2566

329

F 2572

330

F 2577, N 42
[188]Nicholson comments on this line: "*Jamā'a* means 'the community or brotherhood of saints and spiritual men.'"
[189]"The idol of clay" is the "self" which veils man from God.
[190]In Persian literature the world is often likened to an old woman who survives many bridegrooms.
[191]"Was not God's land wide enough that you might take refuge in it?" Qur'an 4: 99.
The prison refers to the earthly involvements which keep man from God.
"Knot care less": Nicholson translates this phrase "Avoid entangled thoughts" or "Do not bewilder yourself by useless thinking."

331

F 2589
[192]In the past it was believed that the earth was encircled by nine spheres.

332

F 2605
[193]For "taking dates to Baṣra," see note 19.
The Sea of Oman was well known for its pearls.
[194]For a description of the game of the *nard* (an Oriental form of backgammon), see Nicholson's notes on the *Math.* 2: 613. The board of this game has six sections, hence the term *šaš dar* or *šašdara* is connected with it. There is an obvious analogy between this game and the world with its six spatial relations, viz., right and left, before and behind, above and below. In this line the "six-sided dice" and "the checker board" and the "human dice" seem to represent the human head (the seat of reason), and the body and the heart respectively. It means that the heart and head, or reason and intuition, cannot be reconciled.

333

F 2613

334

F 2625
[195]This line shows the indifference of the Sufis towards the formal or traditional knowledge taught in the schools of theology. See note 110.
[196]For the Sīmorḡ, see note 180
[197]Qur'an 67: 1: "Blessed be He in whose hands is dominion; and he over all things hath power." This verse is connected with an incident in the life of Moḥammad while he was still in Mecca. One day he was engaged in a heated discussion with the pagans of Quraish about the Qur'an, when an old blind man came in and kept interrupting their discussion as he wanted to learn the Qur'an. At first Moḥammad "frowned and turned away" (Qur'an 80: 1), but then realizing that the man might be hurt, he paid attention to him. This sura asks for more attention for anyone who seeks to know the truth.

335

F 2627
[198]To decorate the outside hall of the public baths with paintings on the tiles was a common practice in Iran.
[199]Arberry had "essence" or "pearl."

336

F 2633

337

F 2641

338

F 2647
²⁰⁰Mount Qāf is the legendary abode of the Sīmorġ, see note 180.
The legend has it that the *būtīmār* (the heron) sits on the shore of the sea but does not drink water lest it may be used up.

339

F 2656
²⁰¹This might refer to the tradition which says: "There is a time for me with God that no chosen prophet or archangel can come between us." This might also be a reference to a legend about the ascension of Moḥammad to Heaven. It relates that when he was about to enter into the presence of God, he said to Gabriel, who was his guide in this celestial journey, "O my brother, why hast thou fallen behind me?" Gabriel replied, "Were I to come one fingertip nearer, sure I should be consumed." Cf. Nicholson, *Math.* 1: 1066-7.

340

F 2664

341

F 2667
²⁰²According to Aflākī *(Manāqeb,* 726-28) this *ġazal* celebrates the marriage of the daughter of Ṣalāḥ-al-dīn Zarkūb with Niẓām al-dīn Ḳaṭṭāṭ.

342

F 2674
²⁰³All the phenomenal forms are "intoxicated" with the Divine Love according to their respective capacities. Cf. *Gulshan-i Rāz,* 825.
²⁰⁴The reference is to the Qur'an (33: 72): "We indeed offer the trust to the heavens and the earth and the mountains, but they refused to bear it, being afraid of it; but man undertook it—he was indeed ignorant and unjust." The commentators of the Qur'an generally regard the "trust" *(amāna)* as the Faith of Islam and obedience to its laws. The Sufis say that it is gnosis *(ma'refa)* or the inspiration of Divine Love, which only man was able to treasure. It is because of this virtue that man is the vice-regent of God and has many of His attributes.

343

F 2684

344

F 2693

345

F 2696
[205]For *Komār* Arberry's translation was "crop sickness."
[206]This line is only in CB.

346

F 2703

347

F 2707
[207]Karbala is a city in Iraq where Ḥoseyn, the grandson of the Prophet, fought against the Umayyad Yazīd and died with his few followers. The city was originated around the shrine of the Imam.

348

F 2713
[208]Qur'an 34: 13.

349

F 2728
[209]"Upon them [the believers] will be garments of fine green silk and brocade, and bracelets of silver; and their Lord will give them to drink of a wine pure and holy." Qur'an 76: 21.

350

351

F 2737

352

F 2756
[210]When Moses asked to see God on the Mount, the answer was, "You will never see me." Qur'an 7: 143.

353

F 2760
[211]In the second hemistich of this line instead of *bāda* (wine) F has *bād* (wind or air) which means: "You are puffed up with pride."
[212]*Sorma* is kohl, an antimony preparation used to darken the edges of the eyelids.

354

F 2775

355

F 2776

356

F 2779

357

F 2788
[213]It was believed that the ostrich eats fire.

358

F 2795
[214]*Suhail (Canopus)* is mostly seen in Yemen.
[215]Musk of Tartary is the best kind of musk.

359

F 2805

360

F 2814

361

F 2820, N 47
[216]In this verse Rūmī refers to the well-known tradition which the Sufi poets often have made use of. God declares: "I was a hidden treasure and I desired to be known, so I created the creation in order that I might be known." Cf. Nichol-

son's notes on the *Dīvān* 4: 2 and 23: 7.

[217]The reference is to the Qur'an 15: 29: "[God said to the angels:] 'When I have completed him [Adam] and breathed of my spirit into him, you will fall and worship him.'" According to Nicholson *rūḥ* (spirit) is probably used here as the reasonable soul *(rūḥ-e nāteqa)*.

[218]*When man contemplates his own evolution—from inanimate to plant and then animal life, and eventually to the state of man—he will realize that he might go further and even surpass angels in his nearness to God. See Nicholson's notes, 47: 12 and 12: 6–10.*

362

F 2828, N 43

[219]When Moses asked to see God (cf. note 209), he only revealed himself to Mount Sinai and made it dust, and Moses fell in a swoon (Qur'an 7: 139). Similarly the base and worldly alloy of man is transmuted by spiritual experience or God's alchemy. In Islamic literature Korah is proverbial for his riches. The Qur'an (27: 76–81) refers to him as a man who has grown insolent and vicious because of his wealth.

[220]In the past, sugar was brought from Egypt. Rūmī says that within you there is a divine element which produces sweetness and love, so it is as if you have a sugar plantation within yourself.

[221]If you realize your own better self, which is the reflection of the divine beauty, you will be indifferent to external beauties.

[222]According to Nicholson the "six wicks" are the eyes, ears, nose and mouth.

[223]The heart as the seat of love is likened to the Kaaba.

363

F 2830

[224]God "has created from water; then He has established relationships of lineage and marriage." Qur'an 25: 54. This also could refer to human sperm. Man was originally one or two drops of water; now he has become a Noah on the sea.

[225]If someone's cap reaches the sky, he has attained a high position.

[226]Qur'an 7: 139, i.e., you will attain such a status that God will not say: "You will never see me."

364

F 2832

365

F 2838
[227]A play on the name of *Shams* which means sun.

366

F 2845

[228]The second hemistich of this line seems to refer to this sura of the Qur'an: "Say: He is God . . . He begetteth not, nor is he begotten."

367

F 2852

[229]The legend has it that by the order of God a gnat penetrated into his brain through his nose and caused the death of this tyrant king of Babylonia.

[230]The reference is to the dog of the Companions of the Cave (cf. Qur'an 28: 9–22) which is the same as the Christian legend of the Seven Sleepers of Ephesus.

368

F 2859

[231]According to the Muslims paradise has eight stages, whereas hell has seven levels.

[232]The reference is to the tradition which says: "The fire [of hell] says to the pious, 'go away, your light extinguished my fire.'"

369

F 2865

370

F 2873

371

F 2880

[233]*Meydān* is a square.

372

F 2894

[234]"Camel-hearted" is a cowardly person or someone who holds a grudge long in his heart.

[235]Arberry had: "Since there is no opening in your head . . ."

[236]Qur'an 6: 76–7: "When the night covered him [Abraham], he saw a star; he said: 'This is my Lord.' But when it set, he said: 'I do not love those who set.' When he saw the moon rising in glory, he said, 'This is my Lord.' But when the moon set, he said: 'Unless my Lord guides me, I shall surely be among those who go astray.' When he saw the sun rising in splendor, he said: 'This is my Lord; this is the greatest of all.' But when the sun set, he said: 'O my people! I am now free from your guilt of giving partners to God.'"

[237]Borāq is the legendary steed of Moḥammad which carried him to his ascension.

[238]*Besmellāh al-rahmān al-rahīm* (in the name of God, most gracious, most merciful) is repeated in the beginning of every sura of the Qur'an. *Besmellāh* is mentioned when a bird or animal is slaughtered, hence the word *besmel* (an abbreviated form of the same) means to slaughter. Rūmī here plays on the two meanings of the word.

373

F 2899

[239]*Nesār-e āstīn* (shaking one's sleeves) is a reference to dancing.
[240]A play on the name of Ṣalāḥ-al-dīn Zarkūb which means Ṣalāḥ-al-dīn the goldminter.

374

F 2902

[241]Qur'an 47: 38.
[242]Qur'an 24: 35.

375

F 2912

[243]*Bī sar o pā* (literally: without foot and head) idiomatically means a person of no importance or standing.

376

F 2916

[244]For *Alast*, see note 160.

377

F 2922

[245]Cf. the prologue of the *Math.* lines 9-10.
[246]The inhabitants of the ancient city of Ray, which now lies in the south of Tehran, used to build their houses underground or with very low doors in order to keep away the invaders. See *Ray-e Bāstān* by Husain Karīmiyan, Tehran 1971, 1: 257.

378

F 2927

379

F 2933

²⁴⁷*Allāh-o Akbar* (God is great) is the call for prayer.

²⁴⁸Mahastī means "you are a moon," or "the lady of the moon," or simply a lady.

380

F 2942

381

F 2946

²⁴⁹For Bāyazīd see *First Selection*, note on 1, verse 21.

²⁵⁰The *Kirqa* (or the robe) of the Sufis usually was blue.

²⁵¹For Mahastī (the lady) see note 247.

382

F 2958

²⁵²"Dusty of face" means humble.

²⁵³The "reversed horseshoe" is a metaphor for someone who reverses the shoes of his horse in order to confuse the trail and mislead his pursuers. Cf. Nicholson, *Math.* notes, 1: 2841. The metaphor could refer to the world as well, see note 260.

383

F 2964

²⁵⁴The line is derived from the tradition which says: "Search for goodness among the handsome ones." F 6: 208.

²⁵⁵Arberry's translation was "Pretty of cheek, annihilate being . . . " The revision into "Pretty of cheek, bring nonexistence into existence" follows Forū-zānfar's text.

384

F 2967

²⁵⁶The splitting of the moon will be the sign of the approaching end of the world (Qur'an 54: 1). According to Nicholson, at an early date this passage was explained as a miracle wrought by Moḥammad in his celestial journey. Cf. *First Selection*, notes on 1, verse 8.

385

F 2981

²⁵⁷According to some Sufis God has created eighteen thousand, and according to some others fifty thousand, worlds. See Sajjādī, *Farang-e 'erfānī*, 327.

386

F 2984

258For "the seven oft-repeated verses" of the Qur'an, see *First Selection*, note on 24, verse 5.

387

F 2998

388

F 3001

259"Nine eyes" is a reference to the nine holes on the reed.

260Arberry's translation was: "O shame of the head, on this way, disgrace, knowledge."

261According to an ancient belief, the earth was on the two horns of an ox. The "reversed horseshoe" here seems to refer to the world. See note 252.

389

F 3019

390

F 3021

391

F 3034

262This line could also be translated: "Bud and flowers came as forgiveness so that you may not see the ugliness of the thorn." *Maǧfara* (forgiveness) could also be read as *meǧfar-at* (your helmet)

263The nomadic Ǧozz tribes invaded and destroyed Khorasan in the twelfth century.

392

F 3038

264For Borāq see note 236.

265For Khidr, see *First Selection*, note on 6, verse 2; also note 34.

266*Rokn-e Yamāni* (the Yemeni pillar), a name given to the southwest corner of the Kaaba which faces Yemen. Cf. Nicholson's note 44: 11.

267For *ṣāheb-qerān* (Lord of the Fortunate Conjunction), see note 137.

393

F 3048

268A tradition says: "The believers are quiet and easygoing like a docile camel, when [God] binds them they accept the bond, and when He makes them sit on a rock they sit." F 6: 261. Arberry had: "who makes his camel driven," a less literal translation.

394

F 3050
[269]Doldol was the name of a mule ridden by 'Alī.

395

F 3051, N 48
[270]The story of a white falcon whose beak and claws were cut by a "wicked old woman" is told in the *Math.* 2: 265–325. The falcon typifies the human soul who has been separated from its divine origin. The "falcon-drum": according to Nicholson's note on the *Dīvān* (16: 3), "When the huntsman wishes to call his bird back, he beats a drum: the hawk, having an affection for the drum, returns speedily."

[271]*Shikūr-e shakūr* if applied to God means "in the search of or hunting for one who is All-Grateful and rewards well His servants." Nicholson, on the authority of one line from Sa'dī's *Būstān*, suggests that "the two wings like a shield" are hope and fear, since the Sufis believe that "fear and hope for man are like the two wings of a bird." Cf. Nicholson's note on this poet, verse 10.

396

F 3055, N 45
[272]For the sleep of phenomenal existence, see Nicholson's notes on the *Dīvān* 39, verse 9 and 36, verse 5.

[273]For the "eye of intelligence," see Nicholson's note on the *Dīvān* 11: verse 5.

F. has *čishm-e kar* which Arberry translates literally as "the ass's eye." Nicholson has *čishm-e kaj* (the eye that sees falsely). The "eye of wrong" here replaces the former version.

[274]Being black or being buried in the dark refers to man's involvement in this world.

[275]*Moštari-ta'a* means a person born under the planet Jupiter which apparently brings good fortune. Another reading could be "a person whose planet is Jupiter when it is in ascension."

397

F 3061
[276]'Oqdat-al-zanab in common parlance is "the knot of Draco" whereas its literal meaning is "the node of the tail" as opposed to "the node of the head" ('oqdat-al-ra's). The former refers to the intersecting point between ecliptic and lunar orbits as the moon is ascending to the north, while the latter is its descending point to the south (cf. C.A. Nallimo, *Opus Astronomicum al-Batamii*, 2: 346; Bīrūnī, *The Book of Instruction in the Elements of the Art of Astrology (al-Tafhīm)* text and translation by Ramsay Wright, London, 1934, 154. Popular

imagination placed a dragon on the lunar orbit which they said devours the sun, hence the "tail" and "head."

[277]*'Azab-ḳāna* is a bachelor's house and metaphorically means a house of loneliness. Cf. F 7: 369.

398

F 3071

399

F 3079
[278]For *'anqā,* see note 180.

400

F 3090
[279]The reference is to the Qur'an 67: 5: "And We have adorned the sky of the world with lamps, and We have made them as missiles to drive away the evil ones."

Bibliography

Aflākī. *Manāqeb al-'Ārefīn* (cited as *Manaqeb*). 2 vols. Ankara, 1959-61. Biographies of Rūmī and his circle, edited by Tahsin Tazici.

Arberry, A. J. *The Rubā'īyāt of Jalāl al-Dīn Rūmī.* London, 1949. Introduction and verse translations.

——— *Classical Persian Literature.* London, 1958.

——— *Discourses of Rūmī.* London: John Murray, 1961. Annotated translations of the *Fīhi mā fīhi*, Rūmī's occasional conversations.

——— *Mystical Poems of Rūmī: First Selection, Poems 1-200* (cited as *First Selections*). Chicago: University of Chicago Press, 1968.

Beatty, Chester. Chester Beatty manuscript Persian 116 (cited as C.B.).

Celaleddin, Mevlana. *Dīvān-e Kabir* (cited as Golpinarli). Turkish translation by Abdulbaki Golpinarli, 5 vols. Istanbul, 1957-60.

Encyclopedia of Islam (cited as *E.I.*) 2nd ed. London, 1960—.

Forūzānfar, Badi al-Zamān. *Aḥādīs̱-e Mas̱navī* (cited as *Aḥūdīs̱*). Tehran, 1955.

——— *Zendagānī-ye Mowlānā Jalāl al-dīn Moḥammad.* 2nd ed. Tehran, 1954. Biography of Rūmī.

——— *Kullīyāt-e Šams* (cited as F). Tehran, 1957-66. Critical edition of the collected odes, quatrains, and other poems of Rūmī, with glossary and notes.

Gowharīn, Ṣādeq. *Farhang-e loḡāt va ta'bīrāt-e Mas̱navī* (cited as Gowharin). 5 vols: incomplete. Tehran, 1959-60.

Iqbal, Afzal. *The Life and Thought of Rumi.* Lahore, 1957.

Jāmī. *Lawā'ih.* Edited and translated by E. W. Whinfield and Mirza Muhammad Kazvīnī. Oriental Translation Fund, New Series, 16. London, 1906.

Lane, E. W. *An Arabic-English Lexicon* (cited as Lexicon). London, 1863-85.

Nicholson, R. A., (cited as N). *Selected Poems from the Dīvāni Shamsī Tabrīz.* Cambridge, 1898. Introduction, selected texts, translations, and notes.

——— *The Mathnawī of Jalāu'ddīn Rūmī* (cited as *Math.*) 8 vols. London: Luzac, 1925-40. Critical edition, translation, and commentary on Rumi's mystical epic.

——— *Rūmī, Poet and Mystic.* London: Allen & Unwin, 1950. Introduction and select translations.

Sajjādī, Dr. Ja'far. *Farhang-e loḡāt va es̱telāḥāt va ta'bīrāt-e 'erfānī* (cited as *Farhang-e 'erfānī*). Tehran, 1962.

——— *Farhang-e olūm-e 'aqlī.* Tehran, 1962.

Shabistari, Mahmud. *Gulshan-i Raz, The Mystic Rose Garden* (cited as *Gulshan-i Raz*). The Persian text, with English translation and notes, chiefly from the commentary of Moḥammad b. Yahya Lahiji by E. W. Whinfield, London, 1880.